From Minnesota ... More than a COOKBOOK

By
Laurie Gluesing
and
Debra Gluesing

Illustrated by
Alvera M. Lundin

Edited by
Gigi Lambrecht

ISBN: 0-9631357-1-6
(previously 0-913703-09-5)

1st Printing: July, 1985
1st Revised Printing: January, 1992

Typeset by Bolger Publications
            Minneapolis, MN

Recipe editor: Betsy Norum

Published by Gluesing and Gluesing, Inc.
            4675 Hodgson Road
            Shoreview, Minnesota 55126

Cover Design: *From Minnesota . . . More than a Cookbook* by Joan &
Bruce Nygren. Copyright 1992 by Gluesing and Gluesing, Inc. Exclusive
distribution rights held by More Than Souvenirs, Inc.

Printed on Recycled Paper

From Minnesota . . . More than a Cookbook is an offering from connoisseurs of good eating across the state. These congenial cooks have shared with us some of their favorite recipes for delectable edibles ranging from daily bread to the more fanciful fare.

We "Gluesing Girls" love traveling the back roads, taking the side trips, and soaking up the flavor of Minnesota. Its rare flair for creative cuisine, happy hospitality and lively lore are a constant delight to us, and we hope to pass the pleasure on to you.

With many thanks to our friends, and in celebration of all the people, places and things which make up our splendid state, we present this collection, our tribute . . .

To Minnesota . . . More than Ever,

Laurie Gluesing

Debra Gluesing

CONTENTS

Prairie Land Breads

It wasn't until the 1950's that it became possible to fabricate a side-weld polyethylene bag with the addition of a gusset giving it a flat bottom, which made it adaptable to the packaging of bread. This side-weld development was pioneered by G. T. Schjeldahl, a Minnesota inventor who recognized its superiority over other styles of packaging in maintaining freshness of the product. The G. T. Schjeldahl Company in Northfield was also responsible for the Echo I and Echo II balloons.

Cracked Wheat Bread

1 package active dry yeast (not rapid rise)
¼ cup warm water (105 to 115°)
½ cup packed brown sugar
¼ cup shortening
2 teaspoons salt
2½ cups hot water
2½ cups cracked wheat
5½ cups unbleached or bread flour

Dissolve yeast in warm water. Combine brown sugar, shortening, salt and hot water in large bowl; cool to lukewarm. Add cracked wheat and 1 cup flour; beat well. Add dissolved yeast and as much of the remaining flour as is necessary to make a stiff dough. Knead on a floured surface at least 10 minutes, until smooth. Shape dough into a ball and grease surface lightly; place in greased bowl. Cover and let rise in warm place until doubled, about 1½ hours. Punch dough down; shape into two balls of equal size; cover and let rest 10 minutes. Flatten each ball into an 18x8-inch rectangle. Beginning at one narrow end, roll toward the other narrow end, sealing at each turn with the edge of your hand. Press ends of loaf to seal and tuck under the sealed strips. Place each loaf in a greased loaf pan and let rise until doubled, about 1¼ hours. Heat oven to 375°. Bake 40 to 45 minutes or until loaves sound hollow when tapped. If bread browns too quickly, cover with a foil tent during the last 15 to 20 minutes of baking time. Cool loaves in pans for 5 minutes; remove and continue cooling on wire rack.

Makes 2 loaves

Note: Cracked wheat can usually be purchased at a food co-op. If you find someone to crack it for you, you'll enjoy this bread even more!

The fabric of Minnesota is woven around the small towns that dot the state. Each town is its own story of the hardship, endurance and joy of turning a wilderness into a home. Nothing makes a house homey like the smell of freshly baked bread. On the frontier, making bread was a regular part of housekeeping, and it was nothing to make a dozen loaves at a time. The following recipe only makes four loaves, but the magnificent aroma is real homebred.

Norwegian Rye Bread
"a taste of molasses"

1 quart lukewarm water (105 to 115°) or scalded milk
2 cakes yeast or 2 packages active dry yeast
2 cups all-purpose flour
½ cup shortening, melted
¾ cup molasses
½ cup packed brown sugar
4 teaspoons salt
2 cups rye flour
4 to 6 cups all-purpose flour

Dissolve yeast in warm water. Stir in 2 cups all-purpose flour, enough to make a soft sponge batter. Let rise, covered, in warm place about 1½ hours until spongy. Add shortening, molasses, sugar, salt and rye flour; mix well. Add 4 to 6 cups all-purpose flour, enough to make a workable dough. Let rise; punch down and let rise again. Shape into 4 round or 5 oblong loaves. Place on lightly greased cookie sheets. Heat oven to 350°. Bake for about 45 minutes, until loaves sound hollow when tapped.

Makes 4 or 5 loaves

There have been only seven earthquakes in Minnesota in the last 120 years. Probably the most severe was the one that collapsed chimneys in Staples in 1917. Minnesota is not quite so lucky with tornadoes, however. With a roar like a speeding train, a full-blown "twister" can destroy everything in its path, or pick something up and leave it unscathed some distance away.

Swedish Twist
"Scandinavian Christmas loaf"

1 package active dry yeast
⅓ cup warm water (105 to 115°)
⅓ cup sugar
½ teaspoon salt
½ cup butter
⅔ cup milk
1 teaspoon grated lemon peel
3 to 3½ cups all-purpose flour
1 egg
¼ cup chopped candied cherries
Topping:
1 egg yolk
1 teaspoon milk
3 tablespoons sugar
3 tablespoons chopped almonds
1 teaspoon cinnamon
Candied cherry halves, if desired

Dissolve yeast in warm water; set aside 5 minutes. Heat sugar, salt, butter and milk to warm. Combine lemon peel, 1½ cups flour, yeast mixture and milk mixture; mix thoroughly. Add egg and enough additional flour to make a soft dough. Knead in cherries. Place in greased bowl, turning to grease top. Let rise in warm place until doubled, about 1 hour. Punch dough down. Divide dough in half; make two 18-inch ropes, twist together, pinch both ends and tuck under. Place on greased cookie sheet and cover. Let rise until doubled, about 30 minutes. Heat oven to 350°. Beat egg yolk and milk together; brush top of loaf. Combine sugar, almonds and cinnamon; sprinkle on top of loaf. Decorate with cherry halves. (Or frost cooled loaf with powdered sugar icing.) Bake 35 to 45 minutes. Cool on wire rack.

Makes 1 loaf

The Twin Cities hosted one of the largest sporting contests in the world in 1991, the International Special Olympics. Under the theme "Victory—Winning Over the World," it drew over 6000 athletes with mental retardation from almost 90 nations. The summer of 1990 also brought athletes to the Twin Cities when the Olympic Festival provided the arena for the selection of U.S. contenders for the next regular Olympian Games. Our state may not be as high as Olympus, but it never fails to reach Superior. And if you prize excellence, you'll carry the torch for this bread, by Zeus! It's nothing short of ambrosial.

Wild Rice Three Grain Bread

1 package active dry yeast
⅓ cup warm water (105 to 115°)
2 cups milk, scalded and cooled to 105 to 115°
2 tablespoons butter or lard, melted
2 teaspoons salt
½ cup honey
½ cup rolled oats
½ cup rye flour
2 cups whole wheat flour
4 to 4½ cups bread or unbleached flour
1 cup cooked wild rice
1 egg beaten with 1 tablespoon water
½ cup sunflower nuts

In large bowl, dissolve yeast in water. Add milk, butter, salt and honey. Stir in oats, rye flour, whole wheat flour and 2 cups of bread flour to make a soft dough. Stir in wild rice. Cover and let rest 15 minutes. Stir in enough additional bread flour to make a stiff dough. Turn out onto lightly floured surface; knead 10 minutes. Add more flour as necessary to keep dough from sticking. Turn dough into lightly greased bowl, turn to grease top; cover and let rise in warm place until doubled, about 2 hours. Punch dough down. Knead briefly on lightly oiled surface. To shape, divide entire batch into thirds, form into strands, braid and place on greased cookie sheet to make a wreath; or divide into 2 parts, shape into loaves and place in 9x5x3-inch greased bread pans. Let rise until doubled, about 45 minutes. Heat oven to 375°. Brush tops of loaves with egg and water mixture; slash loaves if desired. Sprinkle with sunflower nuts. Bake 45 minutes or until loaves sound hollow when tapped.

Makes 1 braided wreath or 2 pan loaves

The plentiful little gopher is Minnesota's state animal. Although he is rather unpopular with the farmers of the state, thousands of University of Minnesota sports fans cheer him. He also appeals to lottery enthusiasts, since his image appears on one of the ticket series to identify the game as distinctly Minnesotan and to symbolize one of the lottery's express benefits: support of environmental conservation. The gopher, needless to say, has a vested interest in preserving the native prairies and grasslands of Minnesota.

Easy Croissants

5 cups all-purpose flour
2 packages instant dry yeast
¼ cup sugar
2 teaspoons salt
1 cup water
¾ cup evaporated milk
¼ cup butter or margarine
1 egg
1 cup butter, cut into pieces
1 egg
1 tablespoon water

In large mixer bowl, combine 1 cup flour, yeast, sugar and salt; mix well. In saucepan, heat 1 cup water, milk and ¼ cup butter until warm - butter does not need to melt. Add to flour mixture. Add 1 egg; blend at low speed until moistened. Beat 3 minutes at medium speed; set aside. In large bowl, cut 1 cup firm butter into remaining 4 cups flour until butter particles are the size of large peas. Pour yeast mixture over flour-butter mixture and fold until all flour is moistened. Cover and refrigerate 2 hours. Place dough on floured surface. Knead about 6 times to release air bubbles. Divide into 4 parts. Roll each part into a 14-inch circle. With a sharp knife, cut into 10 pie-shaped wedges. Starting with wide edge, roll each wedge toward the point. Place on ungreased cookie sheet, point side down and curve into crescent shape. Cover and let rise in warm place until almost doubled, 1 to 1½ hours. Heat oven to 350°. Combine remaining egg and water; brush on rolls. Bake 15 to 18 minutes, until golden brown.

Makes 40 rolls

A picturesque covered bridge provided the gateway over the Zumbro River onto Zumbrota's main street from 1869 to 1922. An imposing latticed wooden truss structure, it was crossed by hundreds of wagonloads of wheat in its day. It also provided a romantic stopping point for amorous young couples until the village council ordered a kerosene lamp installed in its middle. Now the only surviving original covered bridge in Minnesota, it has been retired to the town park, a nostalgic relic of bygone times.

Covered Bridge Puff Buns
"kissed with lemon"

½ cup raisins
Hot water
1 cup water
½ cup margarine
1 teaspoon sugar
¼ teaspoon salt
1 cup all-purpose flour
4 eggs
Lemon Frosting:
1 tablespoon butter, melted
1½ tablespoons cream
1 cup powdered sugar
1 teaspoon lemon juice
½ teapsoon vanilla

Heat oven to 375°. To plump raisins, cover with hot water and let stand 5 minutes; drain well. Combine 1 cup water, margarine, sugar and salt in saucepan; bring to a boil. Reduce heat; add flour all at once, and beat about 1 minute with a wooden spoon, until mixture leaves sides of pan and forms ball. Remove from heat; continue beating about 2 minutes to cool slightly. Beat in eggs, 1 at a time, until mixture has a satiny sheen. Stir in raisins. Drop heaping tablespoons of mixture 2 inches apart on greased cookie sheets. Bake 30 to 35 minutes until doubled in size, golden and firm. Remove to rack to cool slightly. To make frosting, stir melted butter and cream together; heat. Remove from heat and stir in powdered sugar, lemon juice and vanilla. While puffs are still warm, spread frosting on tops and sides.

Makes 20 puffs

Flour production in Minneapolis peaked from 1895 to 1916. By 1900 there were 324 mills, one on every river, and at every railroad station there was a grain elevator. Since Minnesota spring wheat was dark-speckled, the "patent process" was developed to whiten the wheat and increase efficiency. This technical advancement secured Minneapolis' status as "Flour City."

Flour City Buns

½ **cup sugar**
½ **cup margarine, softened**
1½ **cups boiling water**
2 **eggs, well-beaten**
2 **packages active dry yeast**
1 **cup warm water (105 to 115°)**
1 **teaspoon salt**
7½ **to 8 cups all-purpose flour**

In large bowl, combine sugar and margarine. Add boiling water and beat well; cool. Stir in eggs. In separate bowl, dissolve yeast in warm water; add to batter. Add salt and flour, 1 cup at a time, mixing well after each addition. Form dough into a ball and place in greased bowl, turning to grease top. Let rise in warm place until doubled. Shape into rolls or buns and let rise until doubled. Heat oven to 350°. Bake 15 to 20 minutes.

Makes about 24 hamburger-size buns

The Minnesota "Gold Rush" is usually ascribed to the Iron Range and to the year 1865. But in truth, it began seven years earlier on the Zumbro River near Oronoco. By that summer more than 100 miners were working the river. Their sluices were washed out by floods that year, but in an unshrinking display of "mine over matter" they returned the next summer for another try. Alas, they were flooded out again. You'll feel no "gilt" in serving this shortcut recipe on minor or major occasions; you'll find yourself flooded with praise.

"Pan of Gold" Cinnamon Rolls

"strike it rich when you're in a rush"

2 loaves frozen white bread dough
¼ cup butter, softened
½ cup packed brown sugar
2 teaspoons cinnamon
Topping:
½ cup butter, softened
1 cup packed brown sugar
¼ cup milk

Thaw dough; keep as 2 separate loaves and let rise in warm place until doubled in size. Press and roll each loaf out to a 15x10-inch rectangle. Spread each rectangle with 2 tablespoons butter and sprinkle each with ¼ cup brown sugar and 1 teaspoon cinnamon. Roll up starting from the 15-inch side; seal edge. On bottom of each of two 9x9x2-inch pans, spread ¼ cup butter; add ½ cup brown sugar and drizzle with 2 tablespoons milk. Cut dough into 12 slices and place cut side down over mixture in pan. Let rise until doubled in size, 30 to 60 minutes. Heat oven to 375°. Bake 20 to 25 minutes. Remove from oven; turn out onto waxed paper.

Makes 2 dozen

The showy pink ladyslipper, Minnesota's state flower, is anything but a fast bloomer. It takes almost 20 years for the plant to bear its first blossom. The concept of state flowers grew out of the 1893 World's Columbian Exposition in Chicago, was embraced by the Minnesota legislature in 1902, and then turned over to the state's women's organizations for selection. The ladyslipper won by an overwhelming majority over the other contenders. It is rumored, however, that the ballot box was stuffed by one ardent ladyslipper lover.

No-Knead Cinnamon Rolls
"quicker than a ladyslipper"

1½ cups milk
1 cup sugar
1 cup lard or shortening
2 teaspoons salt
2 packages active dry yeast
½ cup warm water (105 to 115°)
4 eggs, well beaten
8 cups all-purpose flour
Filling:
½ cup butter, softened
1 cup sugar
8 teaspoons cinnamon
2 cups raisins, optional
2 cups chopped nuts, optional

Scald milk; add 1 cup sugar, lard and salt. Cool to lukewarm. Dissolve yeast in warm water. Add eggs and 4 cups flour to milk mixture; beat well. Stir in yeast. Add remaining flour, 1 cup at a time, beating after each addition. Dough will be soft. Let rise in warm place 1½ hours. Stir down; let rise again. Divide dough in 4 parts. On lightly floured surface, roll one part into 15x9-inch rectangle. Spread with ¼ of soft butter. Combine 1 cup sugar and cinnamon; sprinkle ¼ on dough. Sprinkle on ¼ of raisins and/or nuts. Roll up; seal edge and cut into nine 1½-inch slices. Place in greased 9x9x2-inch pan. Repeat with other parts of dough. Let rise until doubled. Heat oven to 375°; bake 25 to 30 minutes.

Makes 3 dozen

Everyone's favorite ride, Cafesjian's carousel, rotated for 75 years in the heart of the Minnesota State Fair, from 1914 to 1989. This rare and famous carousel features 68 horses and 2 chariots of hand-carved and painted wood, prized for its realistic poses and finely hewn trappings. The concerned citizens' group, Our Fair Carousel, raised $1.1 million to save the carousel and restore its 1914 appearance. If the carousel's absence at the State Fair leaves your family with an empty feeling, you can visit this cherished artifact at its new home in Town Square Park on the top floor of the St. Paul Center. Then later you can reminisce over coffee, while this classic coffee cake goes merrily round and round and round and round . . .

Everyone's Favorite Coffee Cake

2 packages active dry yeast
1 teaspoon sugar
½ cup warm water (105 to 115°)
2 cups scalded 2% or whole milk
8 cups all-purpose flour
4 eggs
1 cup sugar
½ cup butter or margarine
½ teaspoon salt
8 tablespoons butter or margarine
1 cup sugar
8 teaspoons cinnamon
Frosting:
¼ cup butter or margarine, melted
2 to 4 tablespoons water
Powdered sugar
1 teaspoon vanilla or lemon juice

Dissolve yeast and 1 teaspoon sugar in warm water; set aside in oven that is turned off and warm to the hand, until yeast is very bubbly. Mix in milk and 3 cups of the flour; let cool to warm. Add yeast mixture to flour mixture and let rise in warm oven until high and very bubbly. Add eggs, 1 cup sugar, margarine and salt; mix. Add remaining flour and knead until fully mixed. Place dough in bowl; oil top and let rise in warm oven until doubled. To shape, divide dough into 4 equal parts. Roll each into 14x10-inch rectangle; spread each with 2 tablespoons butter and sprinkle with ¼ cup sugar mixed with 2 teaspoons cinnamon. Roll up; shape into circle, sealing ends together. Place in greased round pan; slash top diagonally with scissors. Oil top of dough; let rise in warm oven until doubled. Heat oven to 350°. Bake about 20 minutes. Remove from pans and cool. For frosting, combine butter, water and enough powdered sugar to make spreading consistency; stir in flavoring.

Makes 4 coffee cakes

The first Swede in Minnesota was considered a foreigner, and as late as 1850 there were only 12 Scandinavians in the state. But around the time of the Civil War there was a great influx, with Scandia being the first Swedish settlement. Today the area around Scandia, Lindstrom, Center City and Chisago is the nucleus of Swedish culture and is affectionately called "Little Sweden."

Mazarinkaka
"Swedish almond cake"

Crust:
½ cup butter, softened
⅓ cup sugar
1 egg yolk
1⅓ cups all-purpose flour
Filling:
½ cup butter, softened
¼ cup sugar
1 (8-ounce) can almond paste
3 eggs
⅓ cup flour
1 teaspoon baking powder
Powdered sugar

Heat oven to 350°. For crust, cream butter and sugar together; blend in egg yolk. Add 1⅓ cups flour and blend well. Press on bottom and 1½ inches up side of buttered springform pan. Bake 2 to 3 minutes, just to set. For filling, cream butter, sugar and almond paste. Beat in eggs, one at a time. Mix in flour and baking powder. Pour filling into crust and bake 35 to 40 minutes or until filling is set. Cool on rack 5 minutes; remove side of pan. Invert onto large plate; remove bottom of pan and invert again so pastry shell is on bottom. Sprinkle with powdered sugar. Serve at toom temperature.

16 servings

Note: Traditionally served with coffee, this can double as a dessert.

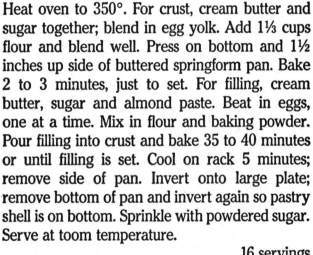

17

"Danebod" means "one who mends or saves the Danes." It was an appropriate name for the folk school founded in Tyler in 1888, because it helped Danish immigrants adjust to life in their new home. Today, the Danish heritage of Tyler remains strong in the Danebod Church, the celebration of Aebleskiver Days and the town's numerous statues of "nissemaend," the Danish elf.

Danish Pastry
"over 100 years old"

Crust:
1 cup all-purpose flour
½ cup butter
1 tablespoon water
Topping:
1 cup water
½ cup butter
1 cup all-purpose flour
3 eggs
1 teaspoon almond extract
Frosting:
1½ cups powdered sugar
3 tablespoons butter, softened
¾ teaspoon vanilla
½ to 1 tablespoon milk
Slivered almonds

Heat oven to 350°. For crust, combine flour, butter and water; divide into 2 parts. Flatten each into oblong shape about ½ inch thick on ungreased cookie sheet. For topping, heat water and butter to boiling; remove from heat and stir in flour. Beat in eggs, one at a time. Add almond extract. Spread mixture evenly on the 2 crusts. Bake 50 to 60 minutes; cool. For frosting, mix powdered sugar and butter; stir in vanilla and milk until frosting is smooth and of spreading consistency. Spread frosting on pastry; sprinkle with almonds.

Makes 2 coffee cakes

Danebod Folk School   Tyler, Minn.

The Finns and Danes who settled in Minnesota brought with them the fundamentals of cooperatives. Theophilus Haecker, called the "Father of the Minnesota Dairy Cooperative," urged the farmers to "treat the cow kindly, boys; remember she's a lady — and a mother." The strength of cooperative marketing helped make Minnesota first in butter production, and most Minnesota dairy farmers can be seen going "overta" the "cwop" after finishing their morning coffee with the traditional coffee cake — spread, of course, with their own butter.

Sour Cream Coffee Cake
"cooperates nicely with coffee"

½ cup butter, softened
1 cup sugar
2 eggs, lightly beaten
1 teaspoon baking soda
1 cup dairy sour cream
1½ cups all-purpose flour
1½ teaspoons baking powder
1 tablespoon vanilla
  Topping:
¼ cup sugar
½ teaspoon cinnamon
½ cup chopped nuts
½ cup butter

Heat oven to 350°. Cream butter, sugar and eggs. In separate bowl, mix soda and sour cream. Add to creamed mixture. Stir in flour and baking powder. Blend in vanilla. Pour into well-greased 12-cup bundt pan. Combine topping ingredients and sprinkle over cake. Dot with extra butter. Bake about 45 minutes. Turn oven off; open oven door and allow cake to cool in oven. Remove from pan; cool completely on wire rack.

Makes 1 coffee cake

Minneapolis and St. Paul share a very special relationship. Like two sisters with different dispositions, they often squabble between themselves, but to the outside world they present a united front. St. Paul is like the noble zucchini: serene, laid-back and mellow. Minne-pineapolis is more upbeat, extroverted and tangy. This loaf unites these two diverse personalities into one compatible entity.

Pineapple-Zucchini Loaf
"for a happy family"

3 eggs
2 cups sugar
1 cup vegetable oil
3 teaspoons vanilla
2 cups shredded, peeled zucchini, well-drained
3 cups all-purpose flour
1 teaspoon baking powder
1 teaspoon baking soda
1 teaspoon salt
1 (8-ounce) can crushed pineapple
1 cup chopped walnuts or pecans
½ cup raisins

Heat oven to 350°. Grease and flour two 9x5x3-inch loaf pans. Beat eggs until fluffy. Add sugar, oil and vanilla; blend well. Stir in zucchini. Stir dry ingredients together and mix in. Stir in undrained pineapple, nuts and raisins. Bake about 60 minutes. Cool 10 minutes in pan; remove and cool completely on wire rack.

Makes 2 loaves

Note: Flavor is best if baked a day ahead of serving.

A cacophonous symphony of huffs, puffs, whiffs and wheezes regales audiences every summer at the multitudes of threshing and pioneer festivals which liven up the state. Antique steam-threshers are stoked up for a spectacular salute to the old days of farming in Rollag, Butterfield, Dalton, Perham, Montevideo and many other towns as they honor their history.

Thresher's Cranberry Bread
"a real stoker"

Grated peel and juice of 1 orange
2 cups all-purpose flour
1 cup sugar
1½ teaspoon baking powder
½ teaspoon soda
½ teaspoon salt
2 tablespoons shortening
1 egg, beaten
1 cup fresh cranberries, halved

Heat oven to 350°. Add enough water to orange juice and peel to measure ¾ cup. Combine with other ingredients until thoroughly mixed. Bake in greased loaf pan about 1 hour or until wooden pick inserted in center comes out clean. Remove from pan and cool on rack.

Makes 1 loaf

21

The phenomenon of "Bonanza Farms" resulted from the vast incredibly fertile lands of the Red River Valley coupled with the new accessibility provided by the railroads. These farms encompassed between 2000 and 30,000 acres of wide open spaces. The massive wheat production, along with the invention of big machinery, an abundance of labor, all the new grain elevators and the giant mills of Minneapolis, made Minnesota the "Bread Basket of the Nation."

Bonanza Bread

1 cup sugar
2 tablespoons shortening
2 eggs
3 bananas, mashed
2 cups all-purpose flour
1 teaspoon salt
1 teaspoon baking soda
½ cup buttermilk or sour milk
Chopped nuts, optional

Heat oven to 350°. Cream sugar and shortening; add eggs and bananas. Stir flour, salt and soda together; add to banana mixture alternately with milk. Add nuts. Pour into greased loaf pan. Bake about 1 hour or until a wooden pick inserted in center comes out clean. Cool 10 minutes in pan; remove and cool completely on wire rack.

Makes 1 loaf

Cloquet has the only gas station in the world designed by Frank Lloyd Wright. It was built in 1956-1957, and is marked by an unusual witch hat roof. He also designed a beautiful Lake Minnetonka home in 1913. Although it was bulldozed in 1972, the rooms were spared to be reassembled and displayed in the New York Metropolitan Museum of Art. Wright always designed buildings to fit the environment, and his structures were enhanced by the the surrounding natural beauty. Here is a blueprint for some delicious self-rising formations that would meet with his approval.

Wrighteous Rhubarb Muffins

¾ **cup packed brown sugar**
½ **cup vegetable oil**
1 **egg**
½ **cup buttermilk**
½ **teaspoon salt**
1 **teaspoon vanilla**
1½ **cups all-purpose flour**
½ **teaspoon soda**
½ **cup chopped nuts**
1 **cup finely chopped rhubarb**
   Topping:
¾ **cup packed brown sugar**
½ **teaspoon cinnamon**

Heat oven to 325°. Combine brown sugar, oil, egg, buttermilk, salt and vanilla. Add flour, soda, nuts and rhubarb; mix well. Spoon into greased muffin cups. For topping, combine brown sugar and cinnamon and sprinkle over muffins. Bake 30 minutes.

Makes 1 dozen

"Our farm was situated in northern Pine County. There were many jack pines around the farm buildings. In spring we'd find trailing arbutus, trilliums, jack-in-the-pulpits, ladyslippers, bluebells, violets, forget-me-nots and many other flowers. In summer, blueberries were plentiful, so much canning was done. Many wonderful aromas wafted about the house as breads, cakes and muffins were baking in the wood stove oven. Oatmeal muffins were favorites."

. . . Willow River Childhood Memories

Aunt Sylvia's Date-Oatmeal Muffins

2 cups uncooked rolled oats
2 cups buttermilk
2 eggs
1 cup vegetable oil
1 cup packed brown sugar
1½ cups chopped pitted dates
2 cups all-purpose flour
2 teaspoons baking soda
1 teaspoon baking powder
1 teaspoon salt

Soak oats in buttermilk 1 hour. Heat oven to 350°. Beat eggs; mix in oil, sugar and dates. Add egg mixture to oats and buttermilk; mix well. Stir flour, soda, baking powder and salt together; add to oat mixture, stirring just until moistened. Spoon into 24 greased or paper-lined muffin cups. Bake 20 to 25 minutes.

Makes 2 dozen

Trilliums

Paul Bunyan and his faithful sidekick, Babe the Blue Ox, have proven to be an effective promotional device and boon to Minnesota's tourist industry. Many towns such as Kelliher, Akeley, Hackensack and Ortonville claim some connection to Paul. Bemidji and Brainerd recognize the gigantic allure of this larger-than-life folk hero with their memorable statues, and Paul adds to his amazing list of exploits that of wooing sightseers.

Legendary Bran Muffins
"satisfying sustenance for your heroic undertakings"

2 cups boiling water
2 cups 100% bran cereal
1 cup shortening
3 cups sugar
4 eggs
1 quart buttermilk
5 cups all-purpose flour
5 teaspoons baking soda
1 teaspoon salt
4 cups all-bran cereal

Heat oven to 375°. Combine water and 100% bran cereal; set aside to cool. In a very large mixing bowl, cream shortening and sugar; blend in eggs and buttermilk. Fold in flour, soda, salt and all-bran cereal. Stir in cooled bran mixture. Fill well-greased muffin cups about ⅔ full; bake about 20 minutes.

Makes 5 to 5½ dozen

Note: Batter can be stored in tightly covered container in refrigerator up to 6 weeks.

The Blue Mounds near Luverne are a mile-long ridge of rocks which appear blue when the sun sets behind them. Historically, they have served many functions. Indians drove "tahtonka," or buffalo, over the edge of this massive bluff to their deaths. Settlers used it as a landmark because of its distinctive formation and coloration. Frederick Manfred built a home in the side of the Blue Mounds in the 1940's. Author of *Lord Grizzly* and *Conquering Horse*, he based his stories on Indian legends and frontier life in the surrounding area. A herd of "tahtonka" now roams unmolested and the native prickly pear cactus grows unchecked.

Wild Rice-Blueberry Muffins
"blue mounds"

1½ cups all-purpose flour
 ½ cup sugar
 2 teaspoons baking powder
 1 teaspoon ground coriander
 ½ teaspoon salt
 2 eggs
 ¼ cup butter, melted
 ½ cup milk
 1 cup fresh blueberries
 ½ cup cooked wild rice

Heat oven to 400°. In mixing bowl, stir flour, sugar, baking powder, coriander and salt together. In separate bowl, whisk eggs, butter and milk together. Spoon 1 tablespoon of the dry mixture over the blueberries; stir remaining dry ingredients into liquid mixture; fold in blueberries and wild rice (batter will be stiff). Spoon into 12 greased muffin cups. Bake 20 to 25 minutes.

The replica Viking ship *Hjemkomst,* meaning "homecoming" in Norwegian, made a journey to Norway in 1982. Robert Asp, designer of the 76-foot ship, spent 10 years of his life in Hawley building it. Although he died in 1980, the "Homecoming" journey was made by his children. Overcoming all obstacles in its path, including a hapless potato warehouse, the ship made its way to Lake Superior, then sailed down the St. Lawrence Seaway and on in glory to Norway. A museum to house the *Hjemkomst* is being built in Moorhead.

Norwegian Flatbrød
"very crisp, thin, unleavened bread"

½ cup shortening
3 cups water
4 cups all-purpose flour
2 cups graham flour
1 teaspoon salt
2 tablespoons sugar

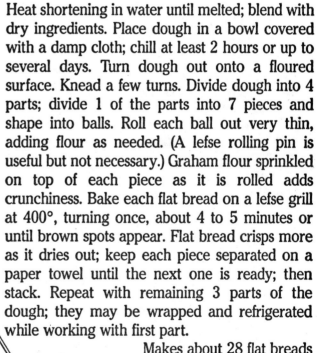

Heat shortening in water until melted; blend with dry ingredients. Place dough in a bowl covered with a damp cloth; chill at least 2 hours or up to several days. Turn dough out onto a floured surface. Knead a few turns. Divide dough into 4 parts; divide 1 of the parts into 7 pieces and shape into balls. Roll each ball out very thin, adding flour as needed. (A lefse rolling pin is useful but not necessary.) Graham flour sprinkled on top of each piece as it is rolled adds crunchiness. Bake each flat bread on a lefse grill at 400°, turning once, about 4 to 5 minutes or until brown spots appear. Flat bread crisps more as it dries out; keep each piece separated on a paper towel until the next one is ready; then stack. Repeat with remaining 3 parts of the dough; they may be wrapped and refrigerated while working with first part.

Makes about 28 flat breads

Charles A. Lindbergh, respectfully known as the "Lone Eagle," made his historic trans-oceanic flight from New York to Paris in 1927. His book recounting the adventure, *Spirit of St. Louis,* won a Pulitzer Prize in 1953 and was later made into a musical. In May of 1985, the Minneapolis-St. Paul International Airport was renamed the Charles A. Lindbergh Airport to commemorate his achievements. The Minnesota Historical Society operates an interpretive center at the boyhood home of "Lucky Lindy" in Little Falls.

Lone Eagle Garlic Cheese Bread
"sends your taste buds soaring"

5 to 7 cloves garlic, chopped
½ cup butter
¼ cup vegetable oil
1 loaf French bread, sliced in half lengthwise
½ cup shredded Mozzarella cheese
½ cup shredded Cheddar cheese
½ cup grated Parmesan cheese

Sauté garlic in butter; add oil. Spread on bread and top with cheese. Bake at 350° for 10 to 15 minutes; brown under broiler.

Optional: Add ripe olives or green pepper slices before baking.

Charles Lindbergh

Dairy Land Breakfasts

On a farmstead near Pelican Rapids is a sight that looks like 25 dinosaurs, each looming regally atop its own hill like an ancient king over his own realm. In a motionless parade of history, they serenely face forward, patiently biding the passage of the eons, oblivious to their own extinction. As you drive closer to this spectral vision, you see that they are in fact prehistoric threshing machines which have been put out to pasture. "Thresher's Hill," as it is known, is a tribute to those majestic old machines which helped to shape Minnesota's early farms. Our individually served "Eggs in a Cup" will give your day a royal dawning.

Baked Eggs in a Cup
"each in its own domain"

Per serving:
- **1 teaspoon butter or margarine**
- **2 thin slices Swiss cheese**
- **2 eggs**
- **½ teaspoon cream**
- **½ teaspoon dry sherry**
- **Salt and pepper to taste**

Heat oven to 350°. Butter 1 custard cup for each serving. Line inside of cup with cheese slices. Open eggs into cup; spoon on cream and sherry. Sprinkle with salt and pepper. An additional slice of cheese can be put on top, if desired. Bake about 15 minutes for soft eggs; 30 minutes for hard eggs.

"The mail must go through!" was the undisputable creed of the dedicated dogsledding mailman, John Beargrease, as he made his runs through Duluth and along the North Shore in the fiercest weather. Today, dogsled racing is just part of the fun of winter sports in northern Minnesota and is always preceded by a hearty breakfast like this one.

Breakfast Skillet
"to start you on your appointed runs"

4 slices bacon
2 cups shredded cooked potatoes (or frozen hash browns)
¼ cup chopped onion
¼ cup chopped green pepper
4 eggs
¼ cup milk
Salt and pepper to taste
1 cup shredded Cheddar cheese

Fry bacon until crisp; drain and crumble. Mix potatoes, onion and green pepper together; fry in bacon drippings until crisp and browned. Mix eggs and milk with salt and pepper; pour over potatoes. Top with cheese and bacon; cover. Cook slowly for about 10 minutes. Cut into wedges to serve.

4 servings

The first cheese was made commercially in Minnesota at Newport in 1852. Hasty had the state's only limburger cheese factory and Pine Island, settled by the Swiss, once had more than 30 cheese factories. Treasure Cave Blue Cheese is aged near Faribault in bluffs over the Straight River, formerly occupied by a brewery. In 1983, Minnesota was second in cheese production in the country. In Minnesota, we love our cheese, and we always smile when we say "curd."

"Say Cheese" Strata
"picture perfect"

8 **slices bread**
   Butter
2 **cups any kind of**
   shredded cheese
6 **slices bacon, crisply**
   fried and crumbled
2 **medium tomatoes,**
   sliced
4 **eggs**
2 **cups milk**
½ **teaspoon prepared**
   mustard
½ **teaspoon salt**

Grease 9x9x2-inch pan or baking dish. Butter bread on one side and place 4 slices in pan, butter side down. Sprinkle with all or part of cheese. Sprinkle with bacon; add tomato slices. Top with remaining bread, butter side up. Sprinkle with any remaining cheese. Beat eggs, milk, mustard and salt together. Pour evenly over bread. Cover with foil and refrigerate 8 hours or overnight. Heat oven to 325-350°. Bake, uncovered, 1 hour, until puffed and golden brown. Serve immediately.

4 servings

Note: Onion, green pepper, sausage, mushrooms, etc. can be substituted for bacon and tomato.

Interstate 90 traverses southern Minnesota from east to west. Around La Crescent and Winona is the Driftless area with its rugged coulees. Going west you pass through the towns in the fertile farming and pork production area, from Austin to Albert Lea to Blue Earth to Fairmont and Jackson. The Coteau des Prairie region takes you imperceptibly 1000 feet higher into the elevated glacial plains of Worthington and Luverne.

Oven Omelette
"a pig farmer's delight"

2 tablespoons butter
7 eggs
¼ teaspoon salt
⅛ teaspoon pepper
⅓ cup dairy sour cream
¼ cup milk
½ cup diced ham
⅓ cup diced Cheddar cheese

Melt butter in 9x9x2-inch glass baking dish. Whip eggs; add remaining ingredients and whip again. Pour into baking dish. Bake at 350° for 40 to 45 minutes. Test with a knife for doneness.

4 servings

The Minnesota Vikings, originally franchised in 1960, is one of the most successful of the NFL teams, mustering vast support from loyal fans of the celebrated gold-trimmed purple and white. Under coach Bud Grant, the team captured 11 division titles and 4 conference championships and played in 4 Superbowls between 1967 and 1983. During these glory years, the formidable defensive line became known as the "Purple People Eaters," and the middle offensive line was entitled the "Fearsome Foursome." Also gaining particular fame was quarterback Fran Tarkenton, known as "the Scrambler." Before he set the precedent, quarterbacks did not scramble with the ball, and he sent officials scrambling for the rule book.

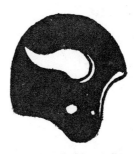

Scrambler Omelette

1 tablespoon butter or margarine
5 to 6 eggs
½ (4-ounce) can mushrooms, drained
½ cup frozen broccoli or asparagus
¾ cup frozen shredded potatoes
⅓ cup milk
¼ teaspoon instant minced onion
⅛ teaspoon seasoned salt
Pepper
1 cup shredded Colby cheese

Melt butter in 10-inch non-stick skillet over medium low heat. Mix remaining ingredients except cheese together. Pour into pan. As bottom of eggs start to set, lift edge with spatula and allow uncooked egg to run underneath. Continue until all egg is set. Divide omelette into 4 wedges; flip each. Evenly distribute cheese. When cheese is melted, remove from pan. Garnish with parsley sprigs or flakes, if desired.

4 servings

Charming to behold and delightful to hear is the Glockenspiel Clock Tower in New Ulm. A creation of the German tradition and one of the few free-standing carillon clock towers in the world, this 45-foot marvel features numerous animated figures depicting old New Ulm. Heritagefest every summer honors the town's strong German tradition with plays, folk arts and crafts, wonderful music and dancing, and that tremendous Deutsch cuisine.

German Oven Pancake with Prune-Raisin Sauce

3 eggs
½ cup flour
½ teaspoon salt
½ cup milk
2 tablespoons vegetable oil
4 strips bacon

Heat oven to 450°. Beat eggs throughly. Gradually add flour and salt, beating well. Blend in milk; batter should be smooth. Stir in oil. Pour into buttered 10-inch skillet or 9x9x2-inch baking dish. Arrange bacon on top. Bake 20 minutes; reduce oven temperature to 350° and bake 10 minutes longer. Serve immediately with syrup or Prune-Raisin Sauce.

3 to 4 servings

Prune-Raisin Sauce

2 cups water
10 to 15 prunes
⅓ cup raisins
½ to 1 teaspoon cornstarch
1 teaspoon cinnamon
½ teaspoon nutmeg
½ teaspoon sugar
Dash of salt

Heat water to boiling; add prunes and raisins. Reduce heat and simmer about 25 minutes. Thicken, starting with ¼ teaspoon cornstarch, keeping liquid not too thick. Add spices, sugar and salt. Add more boiling water if sauce is too thick. Serve over pancakes.

Makes about 2½ cups

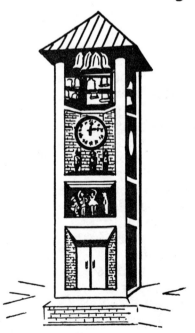

A "starter" dish of "batter-rising" was always on hand in the homes of early settlers and in lumberjack camps. To turn it into a batch of pancakes, it was only necessary to throw in a handful or so of flour per serving and a few pinches of baking soda.

Baked Surprise Pancake

"worth rising for"

7 eggs
1 cup milk
3 tablespoons honey
1 (3-ounce) package
  cream cheese, softened
1 cup all-purpose flour
½ teaspoon salt
½ teaspoon baking
  powder
3 tablespoons butter
  Powdered sugar,
  optional
  Lemon wedges, optional

Heat oven to 400°. In blender, mix eggs, milk, honey, cream cheese, flour, salt and baking powder. Let stand while melting butter in a skillet in the oven, until butter sizzles. Blend ingredients again 1 minute until smooth. Pour into hot skillet. Bake 20 to 25 minutes until puffed and brown. Sprinkle with powdered sugar and lemon juice, or serve with syrup, jam and sour cream or yogurt.

4 servings

If you're an ardent bicyclist, "The Tour of Minnesota" is the race for you. A ten-day, 750 mile itinerary, it is fashioned after the famous Tour de France. You start in the Twin Cities, then go to St. Cloud, Mora, Duluth, Taylors Falls, Cannon Falls, Red Wing, Rochester, Northfield, then back to the Cities. What a glorious way to see the state — if it doesn't rain. This tasty and nutritious breakfast dish will give you lots of mileage!

High Protein Pancakes or Waffles

1 cup cream-style cottage cheese
4 eggs
½ cup all-purpose flour
¼ teaspoon salt
¼ cup vegetable oil
½ cup milk
½ teaspoon vanilla

Combine all ingredients in blender; blend at high speed 1 minute. Bake on lightly greased griddle or in waffle iron.

3 servings

Hiking through the wooded areas of Minnesota, you may notice flattened spots in the long grass, and then realize that you have been following an almost indiscernible trail. If you feel the matted place, it might still be warm from the bodies of deer who rested there, and if you keep your eyes open, you might see a gingerbread-colored streak high-tailing it into the forest. One of our most delightful natural resources, deer and moose in season also provide a popular sport for many hunters.

Gingerbread Pancakes
"dearly beloved"

2 eggs
¼ cup packed brown sugar
½ cup buttermilk
½ cup coffee
½ cup water
2½ cups all-purpose flour
1 tablespoon cinnamon
1 tablespoon nutmeg
1 tablespoon ground ginger
½ teaspoon ground cloves
½ teaspoon baking powder
1 teaspoon baking soda
¼ cup margarine, melted

Combine eggs and brown sugar. Add buttermilk, coffee and water; mix. Add dry ingredients; mix well. Add margarine and mix. Cook pancakes as usual.

Makes about 10 pancakes

Fruit sauces can be made in the blender in any combination of fruits in season, and used to replace sugary syrup as toppings for pancakes, waffles, French toast or even ice cream. Here are just a few suggested variations.

Fruit Toppings

Variation 1:
2 bananas
1 orange

Prepare fruit and cut into large pieces. Combine ingredients for each variation in a blender or food processor; purée until smooth.

Makes about 1½ cups
Note: Sauces made with bananas must be used immediately.

Variation 2:
2 bananas
1 orange
¼ cup raisins, soaked in ¼ cup boiling water
Juice of 1 lemon (about 3 tablespoons)

Variation 3:
3 apples
⅛ cup raisins
¼ cup apple juice

Lake Land Soups

Two weeks before Christmas, traditional Scandinavian households begin the preparation of the codfish for "lutefisk." Washtubs become lutefisk tubs in which to soak the dried stacks of cod for a week. In the "luting" process, a lye solution of critical strength is used: too weak and the fish is tough; too strong and it disappears during cooking. It takes another week of soaking to get the lye out, and then the product is simmered gently over heat until flaky and tender. Often the men stay away from home during this preparation process because of the pungent aroma. But the final presentation of the lutefisk with its complementary dishes of fruit soup and lefse always brings them back.

Scandinavian Fruit Soup
"spicy and fragrant"

1 cup dried prunes
1 cup dried apricots
1 cup golden raisins
2 apples, thinly sliced
1 (2-inch) cinnamon stick
½ cup sugar
  Dash of salt
¼ lemon, thinly sliced
½ orange, thinly sliced
⅓ cup tapioca (or sago, if available)
1 (10 ounce) package frozen strawberries, thawed

Place prunes, apricots and raisins in saucepan; add water to cover well. Bring to a boil; turn heat as low as possible. Cover and simmer 30 minutes. Add apples, cinnamon stick, sugar, salt, lemon, orange, tapioca and juice drained from strawberries. Simmer uncovered until apples and tapioca are cooked. Add strawberries and bring to a boil. Add more sugar if desired. Serve warm or cold, with plain or whipped cream, if desired.

10 to 12 servings

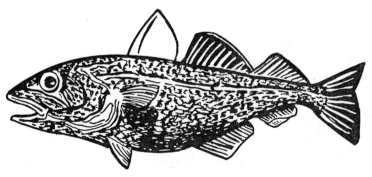

Towering 50 feet high, the famous Split Rock Lighthouse looms majestically above the North Shore Drive near Two Harbors. There it has kept watch since 1910 over what has been called the most treacherous water in the world. A strange magnetic phenomenon occurred which caused compasses to go beserk and sent many a ship crashing onto the perilous reefs. Only beacons flashing every 10 seconds and the haunting call of the fog horn could safely guide ships through these charged waters. New technology made the lighthouse obsolete after 1969, though it still serves as a landmark.

Split Rock Pea Soup

1 pound dried split green
  peas
½ pound bacon, crisply
  fried and crumbled
6 cups water
6 chicken bouillon cubes
2 tablespoons chopped
  mint leaves
2 tablespoons butter
2 onions, minced
1 (12-ounce) bottle beer

Rinse peas; put in soup kettle with bacon, water, bouillon cubes, mint, butter and onions. Simmer until volume is reduced by half, 1 to 2 hours, stirring occasionally. Add beer and simmer 1 hour longer.

6 to 8 servings

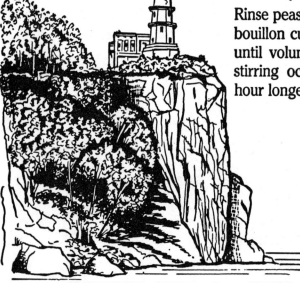

The Red River forms the boundary between Minnesota and North Dakota. This river was once part of the gigantic glacial Lake Agassiz, which was larger than the combined Great Lakes and covered northwest Minnesota, part of North Dakota, and into Canada. Hints of its former shoreline can still be seen. The present day Red River has its source in Breckenridge and runs north into Hudson Bay.

Cauliflower Soup

"you'll want a bowl as big as Lake Agassiz"

1 medium head cauliflower
3¾ cups chicken stock
Salt
¼ cup butter
⅓ cup flour
1¼ cups milk
¼ teaspoon sugar
½ teaspoon pepper
¼ teaspoon ground mace
1½ teaspoon chervil
1 egg yolk
1 to 2 tablespoons cream
2 teaspoons lemon juice

Break cauliflower into flowerets; cook in salted chicken stock until crisp-tender. Remove cauliflower from stock. In large saucepan, make roux from butter and flour. Over high heat, pour stock into roux; stir. Add milk; stir. Add sugar and spices; bring to a boil. Chop cauliflower into small pieces; add to liquid. Bring to a boil; boil 1 to 2 minutes. Remove from heat. Mix egg yolk, cream and lemon juice together. Whip into soup. Serve.

8 to 10 servings

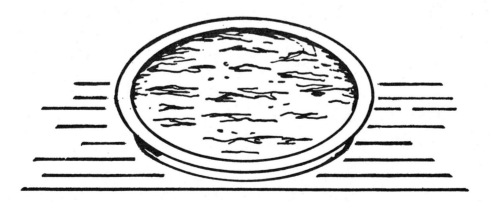

Tomato-Dill Soup with Dumplings

2 pounds fresh ripe
  tomatoes, peeled
2 to 3 tablespoons sugar
2 tablespoons minced
  yellow or green onion
¼ cup butter
2 tablespoons snipped
  parsley
¼ cup dry or ½ cup fresh
  chopped dill weed
  Salt and pepper
4 cups chicken broth
¼ cup flour
3 cups milk
  Dumplings:
1 egg
½ cup flour
¼ teaspoon salt
  Pinch of pepper
1 cup dairy sour cream

Chop tomatoes; sprinkle with sugar and set aside. In large saucepan, sauté onion in melted butter until golden brown. Add parsley, half of dill and all of the tomatoes. Sprinkle with salt and pepper. Cover and cook over medium heat 10 minutes, stirring occasionally. Add broth and simmer 30 minutes. Using wire whisk, mix flour into milk until smooth. Slowly pour flour-milk mixture into soup, stirring constantly. Simmer slowly a few minutes. For dumplings, combine egg, flour, salt, pepper and 2 tablespoons of the sour cream, mixing well. Drop by spoonfuls into soup. Boil until dumplings come to the top. Before serving, put large spoonful of the remaining sour cream into each soup bowl. Ladle in soup and sprinkle with remaining dill weed.

6 to 8 servings

Minnesota is thought of as a Scandinavian state. Indeed it is, if you combine the Norwegians and the Swedes. However, Germans are the largest single immigrant group in Minnesota, concentrating heavily in the St. Cloud and New Ulm areas. This hearty soup will bring out the German in you.

Bavarian Liver Dumpling Soup

4 pounds beef soup meat,
   cut up
4 quarts water
   Few sprigs parsley
   Celery
   Salt
   Dumplings:
1 tablespoon butter
1 small onion, finely
   chopped
6 slices bread
1 egg
1 teaspoon salt
½ teaspoon nutmeg
½ pound calves or young
   beef liver
2 to 3 tablespoons flour

Cover soup meat with cold water. Place over low heat and bring to a boil. Skim off scum that rises to the top. Cover tightly; simmer several hours until meat is tender. Add parsley, celery and salt; simmer 20 minutes longer. Strain and remove fat. To make dumplings, melt butter in saucepan and sauté onion several minutes. Soak bread in water to soften; squeeze out water. Mix bread with egg, salt and nutmeg; add onion with butter. Finely grind liver; add to mixture. Add flour and mix well. Shape into balls; drop into hot soup. Cook 15 minutes.

18 to 20 servings

In the olden days, there was only one threshing machine for many farms, so this chore became a huge community event known as a threshing bee. The men would labor in the fields and the women in the kitchen, and they would move from one farm to the next, all working together until the last farm was done; and then they'd party. This robust cheese soup would make hearty party fare for a threshing throng.

Whole Crew Cheese Soup

36 chicken bouillon cubes
4 to 4½ quarts boiling water
3 cups chopped onion
2 cups chopped celery
2 cups chopped carrot
2½ cups butter
3 cups all-purpose flour
6 pounds sharp Cheddar cheese, shredded
3 (12-ounce) bottles beer

Dissolve bouillon cubes in boiling water; add vegetables and simmer until completely cooked. In saucepan, make roux by melting butter and stirring in flour until mixture is smooth. Add roux to soup mixture; simmer 5 to 10 minutes until thickened. Add about 5 pounds of the cheese and stir until cheese is melted. Add enough beer to make soup consistency, but be careful not to make it too thin. Ladle into individual bowls; top with remaining cheese.

25 to 30 servings

The first brewery opened in St. Paul in 1848. Since then, breweries have come and gone in many towns until today there are only 4 licensed in the state: the August Schell Brewing Company of New Ulm began in 1860; the Cold Spring Brewing Company of Cold Spring has operated since the 1870's; Strohs in St. Paul is the largest family-owned brewery in the nation; and the Minnesota Brewing Company reopened the old Schmidt Brewery in St. Paul in 1991, bottling under the label of Landmark Beer. Modern technology has replaced the old method of aging beer in cutout hillsides or caves, and the once familiar bear "from the land of sky blue waters" has gone to happy hunting grounds. Yet for many, good old home brew still bears up against all competition.

Beer Cheese and Vegetable Soup

2 cups water
2 cups diced potato
1½ cups chopped onion
1 cup sliced carrot
1 cup chopped celery
¼ cup butter or margarine
6 teaspoons instant chicken bouillon or 6 bouillon cubes
½ cup flour
2 cups milk
3 cups shredded American cheese (about 12 ounces)
1 teaspoon dry mustard
⅓ teaspoon cayenne pepper
½ cup beer

Combine water, vegetables, butter and bouillon in large saucepan. Heat to boiling; reduce heat, cover and simmer 30 minutes or until vegetables are tender. Combine flour and milk in small bowl; beat until smooth. Gradually blend into simmering soup. Add cheese, mustard and cayenne. Cook and stir just until cheese melts. Stir in beer; heat through. (Real chicken stock or broth can be used instead of bouillon and water.)

10 to 12 servings

The Northwest Angle, also known as the "Chimney" of Minnesota, is the result of a delightful booboo during the signing of a 1783 treaty in Paris. A misconception regarding the actual route of the Mississippi River gave the U.S. this disconnected piece of land. Roseau is the gateway to the Northwest Angle, which can be reached by Warroad only by boat and is otherwise separated from the rest of the state by Lake of the Woods. Wild rice stands on this small piece of land have been the subject of several disputes with Canadian Indians. Those Indians would probably like to get hold of this recipe, too.

Chimney Wild Rice Soup

¼ cup butter or margarine
1 medium onion, finely chopped
½ pound fresh mushrooms, sliced
½ cup thinly sliced celery
½ cup flour
6 cups chicken broth
2 cups cooked wild rice
½ teaspoon salt
½ teaspoon curry powder
½ teaspoon dry mustard
½ teaspoon dried chervil
¼ teaspoon white pepper
2 cups half and half
⅔ cup dry sherry
Snipped fresh parsley or chives

In large saucepan, melt butter over medium heat. Add onion; cook and stir about 5 minutes until golden brown. Add mushrooms and celery; cook and stir 2 minutes. Mix in flour; gradually add broth, stirring constantly 5 to 8 minutes until slightly thickened. Stir in rice, salt, curry powder, mustard, chervil and pepper; reduce heat to low. Stir in half and half and sherry; heat to simmer, stirring occasionally. Ladle soup into individual bowls and garnish with parsley.

8 to 10 servings

About 8000 Dakota Sioux erected their teepees along the Minnesota River near St. Peter to witness the signing of the Traverse des Sioux Treaty in 1851. This infamous land transaction opened up 24 million acres of land to white settlement when 35 chiefs, in full regalia, ceremoniously signed away their land for 12½¢ per acre. The Sioux Uprising was the eventual consequence, gathering force and finally erupting in 1862.

Sioux Soup
"creamy wild rice"

¾ cup uncooked wild rice
1 tablespoon vegetable oil
4 cups water
½ teaspoon salt
1 medium onion, diced
1 stalk celery, diced
1 carrot, chopped
½ cup butter
½ cup flour
3 cups chicken or turkey broth
2 cups half and half
¾ cup diced cooked ham
Salt and pepper
⅛ teaspoon dried rosemary
Snipped parsley

Rinse wild rice; sauté in vegetable oil. Add water and salt; cook until rice is ¾ done, about 30 minutes. Drain, reserving 1½ cups cooking liquid. In large soup kettle, sauté onion, celery and carrot in butter until onion is transparent; reduce heat. Thoroughly blend in flour and cook 5 minutes, stirring frequently; do not brown. Using wire whisk, blend in hot chicken stock and reserved rice liquid. Cook, allowing to thicken slightly. Add half and half, blending well. Add rice, ham, salt, pepper and rosemary. Simmer 20 minutes. Garnish with parsley.

8 to 10 servings

The call of the wilderness emanates mightily from the **Boundary Waters Canoe Area** in **Superior National Forest.** This pristine wilderness of 2 million acres of lakes and forests includes 1 million acres of preserved canoe routes beckoning to rugged and robust wanderers. Some access points to the BWCA are along the **Gunflint Trail** which starts in **Grand Marais** and meanders through 58 miles of stunningly wild natural beauty; it was once an old mining route. **Ely** also provides points at which to plunge your canoe into the cool waters. Whether you're one to brave the wilds, or simply an arm-chair adventurer, this hearty soup will give you paddling power.

Wilderness Soup

1 pound dry navy beans, soaked overnight
2 quarts water
Meaty ham bone
Salt to taste
5 whole peppercorns
5 whole cloves
2 large carrots, sliced
½ cup chopped celery
1 medium onion, chopped
1 (8-ounce) can tomato sauce

Put all ingredients into crockpot. Cover; cook on low 10 to 12 hours or on high 5 to 6 hours.

8 to 10 servings

Cross country skiing has achieved great popularity in Minnesota with miles of recreational trails now available. If racing is your cup of soup, then the Vasaloppet race in Mora is for you. Initiated in 1973, this is the second largest ski race in the U.S. and routes you through gorgeous woodland terrain including part of the famous Mille Lacs Trail. If stamina is your strong point, direct your skis toward the Minnesota Finlandia Ski Marathon in Bemidji — the longest race in the country at 100 kilometers.

Cream of Winter Veggie Soup

 2 **cups chopped peeled potato**
1½ **cups chopped peeled winter squash**
 ½ **cup chopped celery**
 1 **small onion, chopped**
 1 **clove garlic, minced**
 2 **tablespoons snipped parsley**
 1 **teaspoon dry mustard**
 1 **teaspoon grated lemon peel**
 ⅛ **teaspoon pepper**
 1 **(10½-ounce) can chicken broth**
1¼ **cups half and half or milk**
   Sunflower nuts

Combine vegetables, garlic, parsley, mustard, lemon peel and pepper in large saucepan. Stir in chicken broth and bring to a boil. Reduce heat and simmer 20 minutes. Put 2 cups of the mixture into a blender; purée until smooth. Combine purée with remaining soup mixture. Stir in half and half; heat through. Ladle into bowls and sprinkle with sunflower nuts.

6 to 8 servings

The famous Dalles at Taylors Falls was designated the very first Interstate Park in 1895. Thanks to melting glacial waters it is adorned by bizarre formations in rocky cliffs and potholes up to 30 feet in diameter. The historic W.H.C. Folsom house in the Angels Hill area provides a fascinating tour. This thick and zesty pottage provides an interesting combination of flavors and textures.

Zucchini and Sausage Pottage

"so good you'll want a 30-foot pot"

1 pound Italian sausage, without casing, cut up
2 cups chopped celery
2 pounds zucchini, cut up
1 cup chopped onion
2 (28-ounce) cans tomatoes
2 teaspoons salt
1 teaspoon Italian seasoning
1 teaspoon dried oregano
1 teaspoon sugar
¼ teaspoon garlic powder
2 green peppers, cut up

Brown sausage and drain. Add celery; cook 10 minutes, stirring occasionally. Add remaining ingredients except green peppers. Cover and simmer 20 minutes. Add green pepper and simmer 10 minutes longer. Serve with Parmesan cheese and garlic bread, if desired.

8 to 10 servings

With red feather plumes in their stocking caps, colorful 17-foot-long sashes which they wrapped round and round, ornate deerskin mocassins and leggings, and their characteristic red paddles, the Voyageurs were a flamboyant and fiercely proud lot. They never traveled without their pipes, which became convenient gauges of distance: one pipeful, 2 pipefuls, etc. Their daily fare was not nearly as dashing as their appearance, and consisted of 1 quart of dried peas or lyed corn and 2 ounces of grease, which they'd add to water for soup.

Voyageur Soup
"romanticized version"

2 tablespoons olive or vegetable oil
1 pound Italian or garlic sausage, cut into ¼-inch slices
2 medium onions, chopped
2 large cloves garlic, minced
4 stalks celery, thinly sliced
2 medium carrots, thinly sliced
1½ quarts water
6 beef bouillon cubes
1 (28-ounce) can tomatoes
2 to 3 cups cooked garbanzo beans, drained
1 teaspoon dried basil
1 teaspoon dried oregano
3 medium zucchini, cut into ¼-inch slices
Salt and pepper to taste

In 6 to 8-quart Dutch oven, heat oil over medium heat. Add sausage, onions and garlic; cook and stir until sausage begins to brown. Add celery, carrots, water, bouillon cubes, undrained tomatoes, beans, basil and oregano. Break up tomatoes with a spoon. Simmer, covered, 20 minutes. Skim off excess fat. Stir in zucchini and cook until tender, about 10 minutes.

12 servings

Note: Can be made ahead up to the point of adding zucchini; refrigerate. To serve, heat to simmering, add more water if necessary, stir in zucchini and cook 10 minutes.

The venerable Minnesota Historical Society was chartered in 1849 to collect, preserve, research and interpret Minnesota's legacy. The oldest state institution and one of the most strongly supported, it serves as a model for others in the country. Working in close cooperation with county and local historical organizations, it runs 24 historic sites around the state and conducts tours of the Minnesota Capitol Building. Opening in late 1992 on 10 acres kitty-cornered south from the capitol is the Society's magnificent new facility, the History Center, with six levels to showcase its collections and stage educational and entertaining programs. A state-of-the-art security system safeguards the valuable structure, but with 160,000 pieces of Rockville granite and 29,000 cubic feet of Winona limestone, the building weighs about 200 million pounds. Who's gonna lift it? But do nab this stew for your archives; it has just enough heft.

Hearty Historic Stew
"Rustle it up"

1½ pounds ground beef
1 clove garlic, minced
1 teaspoon salt
¼ teaspoon pepper
1 cup chopped onion
1 tablespoon chili powder
1 (28-ounce) can tomatoes
1 (16-ounce) can lima or
 butter beans
1 (16-ounce) can kidney
 beans
1 (16-ounce) can whole
 kernel corn
 Shredded cheese

Combine ground beef, garlic, salt and pepper; shape into balls and brown in kettle. Stir in onion and chili powder; cook slowly until onion is soft. Stir in undrained tomatoes, beans and corn; heat through. Serve in soup bowls; sprinkle with shredded cheese.

6 servings

Bohemian Flats was a small and poor but very tidy Slavic community which once nestled on the Minneapolis riverbanks where the Washington Avenue Bridge now stands. Settled as early as 1869, it no longer existed by 1931 when this colorful ethnic stronghold was uprooted to make way for progress as developers zeroed in on its prime riverfront location.

Bohemian Stew

2 to 3 pounds beef stew
  meat, cut up
2 cups chopped carrot
2 cups chopped potato
2 cups chopped celery
2 to 4 onions, quartered
3 tablespoons tapioca
1 tablespoon sugar
1 (22-ounce) can whole
  tomatoes
1 tablespoon salt
  Pepper

Combine all ingredients. Bake, covered, at 250° for 5 hours, stirring occasionally.

10 to 12 servings

To bean up for the Minnesota State Chili Championship Cook-Off in Nevis, try this excellent Minnesota chili recipe.

Minnesota Chili

2 pounds ground beef
1 large onion, chopped
2 tablespoons pearl
   barley
2 stalks celery, diced
2 (14½-ounce) cans
   stewed tomatoes
1 green pepper, diced
3 (16-ounce) cans red
   kidney beans flavored
   with sugar
   Salt to taste
   Vinegar to taste
2 teaspoon chili powder

Cook and drain ground beef. Combine with onion, barley, celery, tomatoes and green pepper in large saucepan; cook 1 hour. Add beans, salt, vinegar and chili powder; simmer about 1 hour.

10 to 12 servings

Forest Land Salads

Looming above the Minneapolis skyline and into the clouds is the IDS Center, 57 awe-inspiring stories of glass, steel and plastic. The tallest building between Chicago and the West Coast, its observation deck has 30-mile visibility. The Foshay Tower claimed the status of "tallest" building before the IDS, and had the further distinction of John Philip Sousa playing at its opening.

Fluffy Cloud Salad
"tall taste"

1 (4-serving size) package instant pistachio pudding
1 (20-ounce) can crushed pineapple
½ (10½-ounce) package miniature marshmallows
½ cup chopped pecans
1 (8-ounce) container frozen whipped topping, thawed
1 large apple, cut up
1 (8-ounce) carton cottage cheese

Combine pudding and pineapple; stir in remaining ingredients. Refrigerate.

6 to 8 servings

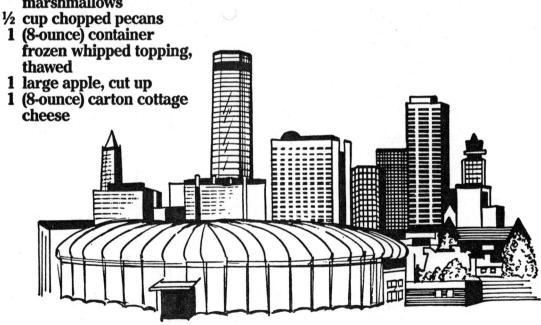

B-6, I-24, N-37, G-51, O-68 BINGO! High-stake bingo parlors with their carnival atmosphere and perpetual action have become a popular and profitable business for Minnesota Sioux and Chippewa Indian Reservations. The first was the Little Six Bingo Palace in Prior Lake in 1982, and the opening of the Shooting Star Casino in Mahnomen in 1991 and the Grand Casino in Hinckley in 1992 brings the grand total to fourteen. Already a multi-million-dollar industry, Indian-owned gaming has burgeoned from the original bingo halls into Vegas-style casinos and entertainment centers with high-tech electronic video games, blackjack, bars and restaurants.

Bingo Salad
"a winner"

2 eggs
2 tablespoons lemon juice
2 tablespoons vinegar
3 tablespoons sugar
1 pint whipping cream
1 cup whole white cherries
2 cups halved white cherries
2 cups cut-up canned pears
2 cups canned pineapple chunks
2 cups quartered marshmallows
Maraschino cherries, optional
Orange pieces, optional
Grapes, optional

Cook eggs, lemon juice, vinegar and sugar until thick; cool. Whip cream; stir in cooked dressing and well-drained fruits. Let stand at least 12 hours.

10 to 12 servings

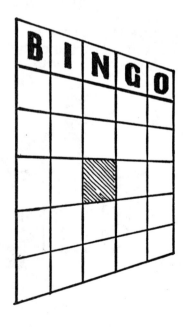

Sweet dreams and charmed slumber are assured to all who suspend a Chippewa Dream Net over their beds. An enchanted leather cobweb icon, it ensnares all encroaching nightmares and holds them until the morning light comes to dispel them. Good dreams and happy visions easily slip through the eye of the web to settle benevolently upon the safeguarded sleeper.

Dream Salad

1 (8-ounce) package
  cream cheese, softened
¼ cup dairy sour cream
2 tablespoons powdered
  sugar
1 tablespoon lemon juice
¼ teaspoon salt
1 cup diced orange
  sections
½ cup halved maraschino
  cherries
1 cup coarsely chopped
  nuts
2 cups diced banana
¾ cup whipping cream

Beat cream cheese, sour cream, powdered sugar, lemon juice and salt together until light and fluffy. Fold in remaining ingredients. Turn into salad mold and chill until firm. Unmold on serving plate. Garnish if desired.

6 to 8 servings

Reflecting Minnesota's dedication to preserving and enjoying historic architecture are the number of wonderful old buildings which have been transformed into lively, exciting, and out-of-the-ordinary retail and dining areas. To name but a few: In St. Paul there is Bandana Square, the Union Depot, and Lowertown. In Minneapolis there is Butler Square, St. Anthony Main, Calhoun Square, the Lumber Exchange Building and the spectacular Riverplace. Duluth has the Depot and Fitgers Brewery. Grand Rapids has renovated an old schoolhouse, and Stillwater's old post office houses many small, charming shops.

Cranberry Salad
"new life for the old mold"

1 (6-ounce) package cherry-flavor gelatin
2 cups boiling water
2 cups cold water
1 (16-ounce) can jellied cranberry sauce
2 cups whipped topping
½ cup chopped nuts, optional

Dissolve gelatin in boiling water; stir in cold water. Let set until partially firm. Beat in cranberry sauce. Fold in topping and nuts. Pour into 8-cup mold. Refrigerate until set.

10 to 12 servings

Fruit Salad Dressing

1 tablespoon honey
½ cup mayonnaise
1 tablespoon raspberry vinegar
2 tablespoons chopped walnuts, optional

Blend honey into mayonnaise with a spoon. Add vinegar and stir until smooth. Sprinkle in nuts. Serve with fruit salad - especially good with bananas, melons and grapes.

Makes about ½ cup

One of our early tourist brochures had a picture of people fishing in a boat. The "catch" was a huge and terrible fish rearing out of the water. The image was so horrifying that it actually frightened Easterners. But even the effect of that promotional over-kill couldn't stop tourism from becoming one of Minnesota's major businesses. Even before the Civil War, the lakes and other natural bounties beckoned, and the cars and highways of the 1920's cinched our tourist traffic. About one-half of tourist dollars spent in Minnesota are by Minnesotans themselves, going "to the lake" for the weekend.

Cool Cucumber Salad
"to take to the lake"

1 envelope unflavored gelatin
2 (3-ounce) packages lemon-flavor gelatin
1½ cups boiling water
1 tablespoon lemon juice, optional
1 (16-ounce) carton cottage cheese
1½ cups mayonnaise
1 cup minced celery
1 cup chopped green onion
1½ cups chopped pecans
½ cup shredded cucumber

Combine unflavored gelatin with lemon gelatin; dissolve in boiling water. Stir in lemon juice. Beat cottage cheese and mayonnaise together. In separate bowl mix celery, onion, pecans and cucumber. Combine all mixtures; pour into 9x9x2-inch pan and refrigerate until firm.

9 servings

Some of the old forest flavor has been preserved by such places as **Rapid River Logging Camp** near Park Rapids, **Tom's Logging Camp** near Duluth, and **Lumbertown** near Brainerd. The **Forest History Center**, operated by the State Historical Society, is located in Grand Rapids. The great white pine was logged in this region in the 1800's, and the Center captures much history of the old logging camps. Another celebrated product of Grand Rapids is Judy Garland, who would certainly be glad to know that her beautiful emerald timberlands are conscientiously being reforested and will not end up "over the rainbow."

Emerald City Salad
"loved by munchkins"

1 **large head lettuce, torn into bite-size pieces**
1 **cup chopped celery**
4 **hard-cooked eggs, sliced**
1 **(10-ounce) package frozen green peas, partially cooked**
½ **cup chopped green pepper**
1 **medium onion or 1 bunch green onions, chopped**
2 **cups mayonnaise**
8 **slices bacon, crisply fried and crumbled**
4 **ounces Cheddar or Colby cheese, shredded**

In a large clear glass bowl, layer all ingredients in order, beginning with lettuce. Refrigerate 8 hours or overnight.

6 to 8 servings

Once a charming rest stop on a prominent stagecoach line, Mantorville has been restored to its 1850's appearance with buildings constructed of stone from its own quarries. Known as a boardwalk town, Mantorville sold individual boards to tourists and locals for $1.00 each, and then installed them side-by-side down the streets with the name of each owner burned into each board. They planned to do the main street only, but the sale was so successful that most of the town is board-walked and includes names from as far away as China and Africa.

Western Salad

Dressing:
1 (6-ounce) jar marinated artichoke hearts
½ cup vegetable oil
¼ cup lemon juice
3 tablespoons tarragon vinegar
2 tablespoons sugar
2 tablespoons minced onion
1 clove garlic, crushed
1 teaspoon salt
½ teaspoon dry mustard
   Dash of pepper
Salad:
   Croutons
2 tablespoons butter
2 heads Boston lettuce
2 heads romaine lettuce
½ bunch radishes
3 ripe avocados, pitted, peeled and sliced

Combine all dressing ingredients in a covered jar; refrigerate overnight. Brown croutons in butter. Tear lettuce into bite size pieces; slice radishes. Combine croutons with vegetables. Pour dressing over salad, toss and serve.

6 to 8 servings

67

Flowers are a precious commodity to Minnesotans because of our short growing season. Many a hardy heart fills with joy when the early-blooming tulips, daffodils and crocuses begin to spring forth after a long winter. A short jaunt from downtown Minneapolis will put you in the bosom of the Eloise Butler Wild Flower Gardens in Theodore Wirth Park, and surround you with the soothing sensation of remote northern woods.

Bloomin' Good Salad

Dressing:
2 cups salad dressing
½ cup grated Parmesan cheese
¼ cup sugar
2 teaspoons parsley flakes
2 teaspoons instant minced onion
Salad:
1 medium head lettuce, chopped
1 medium head cauliflower, chopped
1 pound fresh mushrooms, thinly sliced
¼ pound bacon, crisply fried and crumbled

Combine all dressing ingredients and blend well; refrigerate at least 3 hours or overnight. Combine all salad ingredients; toss with dressing just before serving.

12 to 14 servings

Blue Bells

Driving through the plains of southwest Minnesota, one is mesmerized by what the settlers described as "an endless sea of grass." Sprinkled now with farmhouses with trees planted around them, this area also offers some lovely recreational lakes, including Lake Shetek near Slayton, Lake Okabena near Worthington and Heron Lake near Lakefield.

Cauliflower-Broccoli Salad
"just plain yummy"

1 large head cauliflower, chopped
1 bunch broccoli, chopped
1 bunch green onions, chopped
Dressing:
¾ to 1 cup mayonnaise
1 (1-ounce) package buttermilk salad dressing mix (Hidden Valley preferred)
2 tablespoons sugar
2 tablespoons vinegar

Combine vegetables. Combine dressing ingredients; toss with vegetables. Cover and refrigerate several hours or overnight.

6 to 8 servings

One out of every 6½ Minnesotans has a registered boat. This is the highest ownership of boats anywhere. Small wonder, since we have 2.6 million acres of water to boat on, which is the most surface water of any state. Little Falls is known as the "Small Boat Capital of the World." This easy Italian summer salad makes great boat fare.

Gondola Salad

1 pound carrots, sliced
1 bunch broccoli, cut up
1 medium head cauliflower, cut up
1 pint cherry tomatoes
1 pound pepperoni, sliced
1 (7-ounce) can pitted ripe olives
1 pound Monterey Jack or Colby cheese, shredded
1 medium onion, sliced
1 (8-ounce) bottle Italian dressing

Combine all ingredients; refrigerate until serving.

10 to 12 servings

The beautiful St. Croix River is shared with our gracious neighbor to the east, Wisconsin. Once quite an industrial mainstream supporting sawmills, log traffic and hard-working steamboats, the St. Croix is now a great recreational strip, filled with canoes, motorboats, sailboats and excursion boats. It was the first Minnesota river to be preserved under the National Wild and Scenic Rivers Act. The fall leaves are spectacular along the shores from Taylors Falls through Marine, Stillwater and Afton to Hastings where the St. Croix meets the Mississippi. If you're so inclined, continue on through Red Wing, Lake City, Wabasha, Winona and La Crescent. You will be dazzled by the golden-hued panorama of autumn.

Golden Carrot Salad

6 medium carrots, peeled
  and finely shredded
2 oranges, peeled and cut
  into segments
2 tablespoons finely
  chopped parsley
½ cup orange juice
2 teaspoons honey
  Lettuce

Toss carrots and oranges together in a serving bowl. Mix in parsley. Combine orange juice and honey; pour over vegetables. Serve salad in lettuce-lined bowls.

4 to 6 servings

Do you spend all spring getting rid of dandelions? You can thank Jacob Webster, who moved to Caledonia in 1854. He so hungered for the greens of New England that he sent back for dandelion seeds, thus introducing the prolific "lion's tooth" to Minnesota's fertile soil. He had no idea how it would flourish and spread and become the bane of thousands of yard-groomers. Good Luck!

Dandy Cabbage Salad
"no lyin'"

1 large head cabbage, finely shredded
2 cups sugar
1½ cups vinegar
1 tablespoon salt
1 teaspoon prepared mustard
2 teaspoons celery seed
1 onion, finely chopped
½ green pepper, finely chopped
1 (2-ounce) jar pimento, drained and chopped

Combine all ingredients; mix well.

10 to 12 servings

Paula's Salad Dressing

¼ cup sugar
6 tablespoons vegetable oil
½ cup white vinegar
1 tablespoon catsup
1 teaspoon Worcestershire sauce
⅛ teaspoon red pepper
⅛ teaspoon paprika
⅛ teaspoon chili powder
¾ cup finely diced onion
¾ cup finely diced green pepper

Combine sugar, oil, vinegar, catsup, Worcestershire sauce and spices in saucepan; cook over low heat just until boiling. Fill 1 pint jar with onion and green pepper. Pour cooled sauce over and shake. Refrigerate several hours to blend flavors. Serve over iceberg lettuce wedges.

Makes 1 pint

French Dressing

1 (14-ounce) bottle catsup
¾ cup vegetable oil
½ cup white vinegar
½ cup sugar
½ teaspoon onion salt
¼ teaspoon garlic salt
½ teaspoon pepper
Pinch of salt

Combine all ingredients in blender; cover and mix 20 seconds. Refrigerate 24 hours.

Makes 1 quart

Blue Cheese Dressing
"use Treasure Cave Blue Cheese from Faribault"

4 ounces blue cheese, crumbled
1 (8-ounce) carton sour cream
5 tablespoons mayonnaise
1 teaspoon Worcestershire sauce
1½ tablespoons lemon juice

Garlic salt
Onion salt
3 to 4 sprigs chives, chopped (if available)

Combine all ingredients; mix well. Refrigerate.

Makes about 1½ cups

How does a small town in the midst of a lush farming area come to be an internationally acclaimed medical mecca? William W. Mayo and his sons, Charles and William J., were country doctors in Rochester when a devastating tornado hit the town, wounding many and precipitating the construction of St. Mary's Hospital. From this evolved the Mayo clinic, opening in 1929. The innovative organizational and professional skills of the Mayo brothers immediately attracted an exceptional medical staff, giving birth to another Minnesota success story.

Bacon Dressing
"a whirlwind success"

2 pounds bacon, cut into
   ¼-inch strips
1 large onion, chopped
5 pounds sugar
1 quart cider vinegar
1 quart mayonnaise

Fry bacon until cooked, but not crisp. Add onion and cook until translucent, stirring often. Meanwhile, combine sugar and vinegar in saucepan and heat until sugar is dissolved. Add bacon, onion and drippings; mix. Add mayonnaise; cook and stir until thoroughly blended. Allow to cool slightly. Divide into five 1-quart jars (to distribute bacon evenly put only 1 cup in each jar; then a second into each jar, etc.). Refrigerate or freeze. Before serving, heat slowly until warm - do not boil. Use about 2 tablespoons per serving.

Makes 5 quarts

A man's heart can be won or lost through his stomach. Two government surveyors in the Winona area were certainly a case in point. When they arrived famished in a lovely little town called Rose Hill and found no place there to eat, they spitefully renamed the town Nodine. It has borne this ignoble label ever since, but a recipe like the following could get Nodine back into culinary favor.

Lo-Cal Potato Salad with Sauerkraut Dressing
"no dine specialty"

5 cups sliced cooled cooked potatoes
1½ tablespoons chopped onion
¼ cup chopped pimento
⅓ cup chopped parsley
Sauce:
⅓ cup canned sauerkraut juice
1 teaspoon salt
⅓ cup skim milk
⅓ cup lo-cal mayonnaise

About 15 minutes before serving, combine salad ingredients. In small bowl, combine sauce ingredients and blend well. Toss with potato mixture and serve.

6 servings

The Cuyuna Iron Range was the last of Minnesota's three iron ranges to be discovered. It wasn't until 1904 that a crusty old prospector named Cuyler Adams, along with his dog Una, discovered ore in the Crosby-Ironton-Aitkin area.

Ore-ganic Potato Salad
"an extraordinary range of flavors"

2 pounds (about 12) small new red potatoes, skins on
¼ cup red wine vinegar
1 tablespoon Dijon mustard
½ teaspoon salt
¼ teaspoon dried dill weed
⅛ teaspoon seasoned pepper
1 clove garlic, minced
½ cup vegetable oil
1 cup sliced radishes
6 green onions, thinly sliced
¼ cup chopped fresh parsley
¼ cup dairy sour cream
¼ cup mayonnaise
2 hard-cooked eggs, cut into wedges

Cook unpeeled potatoes in boiling salted water to cover about 25 to 30 minutes or until tender. Drain and slice while warm. (About 6 cups sliced potatoes.) Place in large bowl. In small mixing bowl, combine vinegar and seasonings. Using whisk or fork, gradually beat in oil until well combined. Pour over warm potatoes, stirring gently to coat slices. Cover and refrigerate at least 2 hours or overnight. Gently mix in radishes, green onions and parsley. In separate bowl, blend sour cream and mayonnaise until smooth. Fold into potatoes. Cover and refrigerate for 1 to 3 hours before serving. Garnish with egg wedges.

6 servings

Celebrate! Minnesotans have no trouble finding reasons to rejoice, and there are over 300 festivals about the state every summer season to prove it: harvest festivals, ethnic festivals, art festivals, historical, cultural and agricultural festivals, festivals to pay tribute to famous people or events, to food and other regional products, to fish and other bounties of nature. On almost any day in the year you can find festivities somewhere in Minnesota.

Festive Pasta Salad

1 to 1½ pounds spinach
  fettucini noodles
1 pound ham, cut into
  julienne strips
2 medium tomatoes, cut
  into wedges
2 medium zucchini, sliced
½ cup sliced carrot
½ cup sliced celery
¾ pound cheese, shredded
3 hard-cooked eggs,
  quartered
Dressing:
1 (16-ounce) bottle Italian
  dressing
2 tablespoons Dijon
  mustard
2 tablespoons grated
  Parmesan cheese

Cook noodles according to package directions. Cool; toss with ham, tomatoes, zucchini, carrot and celery. Mix in cheese. In separate bowl, combine dressing ingredients; toss with noodles and vegetables. Divide onto 6 serving plates; garnish with egg wedges.

6 servings

"Gavia Immer," the Norwegian name for the loon, means "wild, sad cry." This only begins to describe the amazing sounds of our state bird, sometimes startling as they slice through the quiet depths of the night. The loon is very competent in water and air — unexcelled in strength and speed while swimming and deep diving, and capable of exeeding 60 m.p.h. while flying. On land, it is quite comical — yes, loony — but you will seldom see one there. It is heartwarming to see the newborn fuzzy brown babies riding on their mother's back or frolicking securely between the wings of both parents, who mate for life. The loon, once an endangered species, has become a beloved symbol of the unspoiled beauty of Minnesota's lakelands.

Wild Rice Summer Salad

2½ cups cooked wild rice
    (about ¾ cup uncooked)
1 (8-ounce) can pineapple
    chunks, drained
2 cups chopped celery
1 cup halved green
    grapes
¾ cup coarsely chopped
    cashew nuts or almonds
2½ cups cut-up cooked
    chicken or turkey
¾ cup mayonnaise
½ cup chopped chutney
    (Crosse & Blackwell
    preferred)
½ teaspoon salt

Toss rice, pineapple, celery, grapes, nuts and chicken together. Combine mayonnaise, chutney and salt. Toss with rice mixture. Cover and refrigerate several hours.

8 to 10 servings

Old hotels are often the most charming structures in a town because they were originally designed to exude an aura of inviting hospitality and warmth, enhanced by time. Minnesota has fine examples, and many are being restored for use as hotels, such as the Anderson House in Wabasha, the St. James Hotel in Red Wing, the Calumet Hotel in Pipestone, the Schumacher Hotel in New Prague, the Palmer House in Sauk Centre, the Archer House in Northfield and the St. Paul Hotel in St. Paul. Many others are being opened and operated as restaurants only.

Restoration Chicken Salad
"very hospitable"

9 cups diced cooked chicken
1 cup flaked tuna
4½ cups diced celery
4 hard-cooked eggs, chopped
1 green pepper, diced
1 (2-ounce) jar pimento, drained and chopped
1 large onion, diced
1 cup sweet pickle relish, drained
Salt and pepper to taste
2 (7-ounce) packages shell macaroni, cooked and drained
Dressing:
3 cups salad dressing
2 tablespoons lemon juice
3 tablespoons cream
1 tablespoon salt
½ teaspoon pepper

Gently mix salad ingredients. Combine dressing ingredients; stir in. Refrigerate.

36 servings

Theatre buffs in the Twin Cities find their heads spinning with the amazing variety of choices in quality stage productions — upwards of 25 on any given weekend. These dramatic offerings range from the famed Guthrie and other equity theatres such as Cricket, to numerous fine community theatres like Chimera and Theatre in the Round, to the nation's largest dinner theatre, the Chanhassen, and a host of exciting smaller and more experimental companies. Twin Citians understand the maxim, "All the world's a stage."

Chicken Curry Salad

Dressing:
- ¼ cup lemon yogurt
- ¼ cup mayonnaise
- 1 teaspoon lemon juice
- 2 tablespoons grated onion
- 2 teaspoons curry powder
- ¼ teaspoon salt

Salad:
- 2 cups cut-up cooked chicken
- ½ cup roasted peanuts
- ½ cup raisins
- ½ cup chopped celery
- ½ cup chopped green pepper
- ¼ cup shredded coconut Iceberg lettuce leaves

Combine all dressing ingredients. Toss all salad ingredients except lettuce with dressing. Serve in lettuce-lined bowls.

6 servings

Minnesota's creative climate has nothing to do with the weather. The Twin Cities are known nationally as an innovative and strong cultural nucleus, nurtured by the joint support of public and private financing. This radiates out and is reflected by the rest of the state in a richly pervasive and on-going love of the arts. Make your next meal creative with this unusual salad.

Chicken-Avocado-Grapefruit Salad

1½ cups diced cooked chicken
⅔ cup cooked long-grain rice
2 grapefruit, peeled and cut into segments
2 to 3 teaspoons finely chopped onion
2 carrots, peeled and cut into 2-inch strips
Salt and pepper
1 large avocado
2 tablespoons French dressing
2 tablespoons lemon juice
Lettuce leaves
6 tablespoons mayonnaise
½ teaspoon curry powder

Combine chicken, rice, grapefruit, onion, carrots and salt and pepper to taste. Peel and dice avocado; mix with French dressing and 1 tablespoon of the lemon juice. Add to salad and toss gently. Arrange lettuce on serving plate; spoon on salad. Mix remaining lemon juice with mayonnaise and curry powder; spoon over salad.

4 servings

The quality of life in Minnesota rated a cover story in nothing less than *Time Magazine* on August 13, 1973. The image projected by *Time* was one of a successful state with clean and honest politics, courteous and fair citizens, balanced and diverse economy, a high living standard, good transportation, excellent schools, quality public services and a real concern for environment. Not only can you live better in Minnesota, you can also live longer. The average life span is 75; only people in Hawaii live longer. Blessed with plenty of clean air, bounteous lakes, and this great recipe for Healthy Tuna Salad, what better place to be than in Minnesota.

Healthy Tuna Salad
"especially good in pocket bread"

1 (6½-ounce) can tuna, drained
¼ cup chopped cucumber
¼ cup slivered almonds
⅓ cup raisins
2 ounces American cheese, cubed
2 tablespoons mayonnaise

Mix all ingredients together.

3 to 4 servings

Note: If you use water-pack tuna, and low-fat cheese and mayonnaise, this salad has only 230 calories per serving.

Variation: Separate 1 can of refrigerated crescent rolls into triangles. Place tuna mixture in center of triangle; fold over to seal and brush with butter. Bake at 375° for 10 to 13 minutes.

Mining Land Main Dishes

Fergus Falls, an All-American town, has a peaceful and rather quaint atmosphere, but there is power behind the scenes. The heat discharged by their power plant into the surrounding water keeps ice from forming even in the dead of winter. The resulting open waters invite the year-round quack, splash and flutter of ducks and geese which would otherwise be forced south. Fergus Falls, Alexandria and Rochester all allow their waterfowl to defy the seasons in this way.

Gold Duck
"richly succulent"

1 **duck, quartered**
  Salt and pepper to taste
1 **(20-ounce) can crushed**
  pineapple
2 **tablespoons butter**
½ **cup white wine**
1 **tablespoon vinegar**

Rub duck with salt and pepper. Roast uncovered, skin side down, at 325° for 30 minutes. Turn duck over and roast until tender, 2 to 2½ hours longer. Drain pineapple, reserve juice; sauté in butter until golden. Arrange pineapple around duck on serving platter. Pour pineapple juice into sauté pan and stir until browned bits of pineapple are loosened; cook until almost caramelized. Stir in wine and vinegar; bring just to a boil. Pour over duck and serve.

2 servings

Minnesota provides a harmonious environment for a vast chorus of cheeps, chirps, tweets, peeps, trills, twitters, warbles, whistles, honks, quacks and other forms of birdsong. Some of the more unusual among the feathered friends who sing our state's praises are the 34,000 Canadian geese that land in the open waters at Silver Lake Park in Rochester. Arriving in the fall and leaving in the spring, these hardy fowl think our winters are fair. In 1983 we could boast 125 pairs of bald eagles, a bare-headed tribute from the majestic lord of the skies. Great Blue Herons have one of their largest nesting

continued on next page

Pleasant Pheasant I

2 pheasants, cut up
Bread crumbs
Margarine
1 cup mayonnaise
5 teaspoons cumin
½ cup cream
2 (4-ounce) cans
mushrooms
Salt and pepper

Roll pheasant pieces in crumbs; pan-fry in margarine until browned. Place pheasant in baking dish. Combine mayonnaise, cumin, cream, mushrooms and salt and pepper to taste; pour over pheasant. Bake at 350° for 2 hours.

4 servings

colonies in North America near Cold Spring, and the cliff swallows that have migrated the same route to Peru for centuries always return to their hearts' home in the beautiful sandstone river bluffs near Dresbach. Hawk Ridge in Duluth is on the east end of the Skyline Parkway, and in the autumn this is a great place to watch the migrating hawks and eagles. Another migrating variety, known as the "Snowbird," is the Minnesotan with the motorhome who heads to Arizona, Florida, Texas and other points south for the winter. But Minnesota always calls them back!

Pleasant Pheasant II

4 pheasant breasts, halved and boned
Salt and pepper, to taste
Flour
½ cup butter
1 small onion, chopped
1 (4-ounce) can mushrooms, drained
1 (10¾-ounce) can cream of chicken soup
1 (10¾-ounce) can cream of mushroom soup
1 (10½-ounce) can chicken broth
⅓ cup sherry

Season breasts with salt and pepper; dredge in flour. Melt butter in skillet; brown pheasant. Remove pheasant and place in casserole. In same skillet, lightly brown onion and mushrooms; mix with soups and sherry. Pour mixture over pheasant. Bake, covered, at 325° for 2½ hours. Serve with wild rice.

8 servings

Much of the economic stability of Minnesota is based on diversity. Although farming is still the #1 industry in the state, the high-tech computer world is close behind. Other important fields are food and related products, finance and insurance, and retail marketing. Minnesota has provided the necessary resources for many of its homebred infant industries to grow to national and multi-national maturity. A few grown-up names that you may recognize: 3M Company, Control Data, Sperry-Univac, Carlson Company, General Mills, Pillsbury, St. Paul Companies, Sears, Daytons and many more.

High-Tech Chicken
"keeps you abreast of the times"

1 (4-ounce) package dried beef
8 strips bacon, partially-cooked
4 whole chicken breasts, halved, skinned and boned
1 (10¾-ounce) can cream of mushroom soup
1 cup diary sour cream

Line 13x9x2-inch casserole with dried beef. Wrap 1 strip of bacon around each chicken breast half; place in casserole. Combine soup and sour cream; pour over chicken. Cover casserole with foil. Bake at 325° for 2 hours; uncover casserole and bake 1 hour longer.

8 servings

Lake Minnetonka has always had the reputation of being a "party lake." In the 1880's, Wayzata and Excelsior had some of the ritziest resorts around. Now the large hotels have been replaced by private homes, each enjoying a small span of the 250 miles of lakefront created by the many bays and islands on this 12-mile-long lake. The Dakota Indians used the shores as a sacred burial ground long before the white man recognized its power. The name means "Large Lake Lost in a Great Piece of Forest." The lost was found by Alexander Ramsey in 1822.

Chicken Minnetonka
"elegant and easy"

2 whole chicken breasts, halved, skinned and boned
¼ cup butter
1 teaspoon dried rosemary, crushed
2 teaspoons chopped chives
¼ teaspoon pepper
1 (8-ounce) can refrigerated crescent rolls
1 tablespoon flour
1 (4-ounce) can sliced mushrooms
¼ to ⅓ cup dry white wine
½ cup dairy sour cream

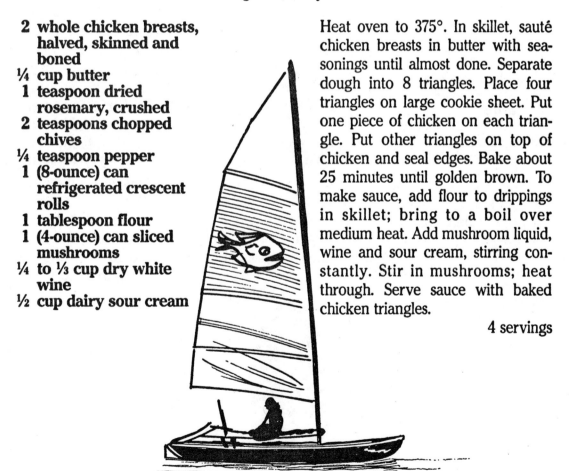

Heat oven to 375°. In skillet, sauté chicken breasts in butter with seasonings until almost done. Separate dough into 8 triangles. Place four triangles on large cookie sheet. Put one piece of chicken on each triangle. Put other triangles on top of chicken and seal edges. Bake about 25 minutes until golden brown. To make sauce, add flour to drippings in skillet; bring to a boil over medium heat. Add mushroom liquid, wine and sour cream, stirring constantly. Stir in mushrooms; heat through. Serve sauce with baked chicken triangles.

4 servings

One word that describes the logging era is BIG. The forests were big, the trees were big, the lumberjacks were big, the tales were big, the business minds were big and they made big money. Stillwater was the lumber capital from 1850-1900. Marine-on-the-St. Croix had the first commercial sawmill in 1839. The St. Croix Boom Company had the largest log boom in the United States, and is now on the National Register of Historic Sites. Lumbering peaked in 1905 and by 1920 the fast and easy cuts were gone.

Broccoli and Chicken Crepes
"tree-top tall taste"

Crepes:
1 cup milk
3 eggs, well beaten
¾ cup flour
1 tablespoon sugar
¼ teaspoon salt
Filling:
6 tablespoons butter
⅓ cup flour
1 teaspoon salt
Dash of pepper
1½ cups chicken broth
1 cup half and half
3 cups cubed cooked chicken
8 to 10 ounces cut-up broccoli, cooked and drained
¼ cup toasted slivered almonds

For crepes, beat milk into eggs. Stir dry ingredients together; stir into egg mixture. In crepe pan or lightly greased skillet over low heat, spoon 2 tablespoons batter; spread into circle with back of spoon. When lightly browned, turn and bake other side. Cool on a towel. For filling, melt butter; stir in flour, salt and pepper. Add broth and cream slowly. Cook, stirring constantly until thick and bubbly. Stir in chicken and broccoli. To assemble: Put spoonful of filling on each crepe. Roll up and place seam-side down in single layer in 13x9x2-inch casserole. Spoon remainder of mixture on top of crepes and sprinkle with almonds. Bake at 350° for 20 to 25 minutes.

8 to 10 servings

The arrival of a considerable Southeast Asian population into the Minnesota ethnic scene has opened up a wide range of new cultural adventures. St. Paul has one of the largest Hmong concentrations of any city in the United States. Their needlework is considered some of the finest in the world. Although the following is not a Hmong recipe, it is a favorite among us.

Walnut Chicken Oriental

"easy stir-fry"

2 tablespoons cornstarch
1 tablespoon red wine vinegar
1 tablespoon cooking sherry
2 tablespoons soy sauce
1 tablespoon sugar
4 chicken breasts, cut up
½ cup chopped walnuts
¾ to 1 pound fresh broccoli, chopped
6 stalks celery, chopped
1 green pepper, chopped
8 ounces fresh mushrooms, chopped
4 green onions, chopped
1 cup chicken bouillon

Mix cornstarch, vinegar, sherry, soy sauce and sugar. Marinate chicken in mixture 1 hour. Heat oil in wok or skillet; roast walnuts and remove from pan (watch closely, they brown fast!). Fry chicken until it turns white; remove. Stir-fry vegetables, starting with broccoli, celery and green pepper, then mushrooms and onions. Add walnuts, chicken, marinade and desired amount of bouillon; heat through.

4 to 6 servings

Note: About 1½ to 2 cups leftover cooked turkey may be substituted for chicken.

Many Minnesotans got a kick out of the Kicks during their heyday at the Metropolitan Stadium. Tailgate parties in the parking lot primed the audience for a rowdy game. But the Kicks, the Strikers and the outdoor stadium are all a thing of the past. The "Met" is now replaced by the Mall of America, the world's largest indoor mall. However, many of the international cast of former Kicks/Strikers players found Minnesota so congenial that they stayed and adopted our state as their new home. This just goes to show that, even though we lack a professional soccer team, when it comes to quality of life, we really can't kick.

Kickin' Chicken Hot Dish
"tail-gater specialty"

2 chicken bouillon cubes
1 cup chicken broth
1 cup cooked rice
½ cup mayonnaise
¾ cup cooked celery (reserve juice)
1 (10¾-ounce) can cream of chicken soup
2 to 3 cups cut-up cooked chicken
2 hard-cooked eggs, chopped
1 teaspoon lemon juice
½ teaspoon salt
Pepper
1 (8-ounce) can sliced water chestnuts, drained, optional
Crushed potato chips
Slivered almonds

Dissolve bouillon in broth. Combine with remaining ingredients except potato chips and almonds. Pour into lightly greased 13x9x2-inch casserole. Cover; refrigerate overnight. Bake at 350° for 45 minutes. Add celery juice if necessary while baking. Remove from oven and sprinkle with potato chips and almonds.

8 servings

A Los Angeles newspaper in the 1960's advised California men: If you want a good wife, don't get a California gal, go to Minnesota. Our good-looking women are still cooking.

California Casserole Minnesota Style

4 chicken breasts or 1 frying chicken
1 dozen corn tortillas
8 ounces Monterey Jack cheese, shredded
8 ounces sharp Cheddar cheese, shredded
Sauce:
1 (10¾-ounce) can cream of mushroom soup
1 (10¾-ounce) can cream of chicken soup
½ cup chicken broth
3 to 4 tablespoons green chile salsa
1 (15-ounce) can chili without beans
1 onion, chopped

Cook chicken; cut into bite-size pieces. Cut tortillas 1 inch wide and in half. Layer chicken and tortillas in 3-quart casserole. Combine sauce ingredients; pour over chicken and tortillas. Sprinkle with cheeses. Bake, covered, 15 minutes; uncover and bake 30 minutes longer.

6 to 8 servings

Wild rice is the only grain indigenous to the North American continent, and 65% of natural stands are in Minnesota. It is fitting that it became the state grain in 1977. Originally harvested only by Indians, "manomin" provided a staple part of their diets, and harvesting from their canoes and processing the rice was a way of life. Even now the Department of Natural Resources protects the natural stands by allowing them to be harvested only in the traditional Indian way, thus ensuring that seeds will fall back into the water for the next year's crop. Commercial sales began in the 16th century between Indians and fur traders, yet several hundred years later, in the 1940's, only about 10% of indigenous rice was being harvested. By 1959, however, all of this aquatic grass was being harvested and consumed, bringing prices as high as $5.00 a pound. Rice blends were created by Minnesotan Sherman Holbert of the Mille Lacs Lake area and sold to Uncle Ben's, giving wild rice wide distribution and popularity. Soon commercially grown wild rice became essential. Research was done by the University of Minnesota on new strains and wild rice paddies appeared around Bemidji and in other areas of Minnesota. Because of certain limitations, Minnesota may not remain the #1 producer of commercially-grown wild rice, but indigenous wild rice will always be a Minnesota claim to fame.

Baked Wild Rice and Chicken
"a claim to fame"

1 cup uncooked wild rice
1 envelope dry onion soup mix
1 (2½-pound) chicken, cut into eighths
Salt and pepper to taste
1 (10¾-ounce) can cream of mushroom or cream of chicken soup
⅔ cup water
⅔ cup milk
2 to 3 tablespoons soy sauce

Rinse rice in warm water. Cover with hot water and let stand 1 hour. Sprinkle soup mix in bottom of greased 13x9x2-inch pan. Drain rice and place on top of dry soup mix. Salt and pepper chicken, place over rice, skin side up, in a single layer. Combine soup, water, milk and soy sauce; pour over chicken. Bake, uncovered, at 300° for 2 hours. Add more water, if needed, near end of baking time.

6 to 8 servings

Note: ½ cup chopped onion and 1 to 2 cups diced celery, sautéed, and ½ cup sliced mushrooms can be added to cream soup mixture.

Wild Rice, "MANOMIN"

EASY TO PREPARE

Stovetop: Wash 1 cup uncooked wild rice thoroughly. Add to 3 cups boiling water, salted to taste, in heavy saucepan. Return water to boil; stir. Reduce heat and simmer, covered, 30-45 minutes or just until kernels puff open. Uncover. Fluff with table fork. Simmer 5 additional minutes. Drain any excess liquid. For chewier texture cook for less time. Yield: 3-4 cups cooked wild rice.

Oven: Wash 1 cup uncooked wild rice thoroughly. Combine with 3 cups water in a covered 2-quart casserole. Cover and bake at 350°F. for 1 hour. Check wild rice. Add more water if needed and fluff with a fork. Continue baking for ½ hour. Wild rice should be moist, not dry. Yield: 3-4 cups cooked wild rice.

Microwave: Wash 1 cup uncooked wild rice thoroughly. Combine with 3 cups water in a covered 2-quart glass casserole. Microwave on HIGH for 5 minutes. Microwave on MEDIUM (50% power) for 30 minutes. Let stand 10 to 15 minutes; drain. Yield: 3-4 cups cooked wild rice.

NOTES

Nutritional Benefits: Wild rice is a natural food — with no additives and no preservatives. It contains high quality protein, is low in fat and high in fiber. Wild rice is an excellent source of B vitamins and is mineral-rich, particularly in zinc and potassium. A low-calorie carbohydrate, one cup of cooked wild rice contains only 130 calories.

Modern processing techniques provide a clean flavorful grain. When identically processed there are no differences in the cooking characteristics and nutritional value of wild rice grown in paddies or in lakes and rivers.

Shelf life: Uncooked wild rice will keep almost indefinitely. Cooked and well drained, it can be stored up to two weeks in the refrigerator. Freeze for longer storage. For your convenience it can be made ahead and reheated in a microwave oven.

Economy: Wild rice expands 3 to 4 times when cooked. Six ounces raw wild rice equals one cup, uncooked, and yields 3 to 4 cups when cooked. One pound of uncooked wild rice measures 2⅔ cups and will yield 8 to 10 cups cooked. Depending on use, one pound (450 grams) will provide 20-30 servings. Its cost-per-serving makes wild rice an affordable addition to your year-round menus.

Thanksgiving celebrations would not be the same if not for Minnesota, the second biggest supplier of turkeys in the United States. These turkeys trot mainly in the plains of Paynesville, Frazee, Worthington, Pelican Rapids and Willmar, and from there into this excellent risotto, which is sure to be gobbled up by turkey connoisseurs any day of the year.

Turkey Risotto
"thrifty and delicious"

Rice Crust:
4 egg whites, stiffly beaten
3 cups cooked, flavored rice
4 tablespoons parsley flakes
Filling:
1 small onion, chopped
1 cup sliced celery
½ green pepper, diced
1 (20-ounce) bag frozen cut broccoli
1 frozen turkey roast with gravy, cooked and cubed
Italian seasoning
Salt and pepper to taste
1 cup shredded Monterey Jack cheese
4 egg yolks
1 cup shredded Cheddar cheese
Sliced almonds

Heat oven to 375°. For crust, combine egg whites, rice and parsley. Spread evenly on botton and up sides of 2 well-greased 9-inch glass pie plates. Bake 5 minutes; let cool slightly before filling. In large skillet, sauté onion, celery and green pepper in butter until brown. Thaw and separate broccoli by rinsing with cold water. Add turkey, gravy and broccoli to skillet. Season generously with Italian seasoning, salt and pepper. Just before removing mixture from heat, stir in slightly beaten egg yolks. Continue stirring until yolks thicken liquid in skillet. Remove from heat and divide mixture evenly between 2 pie shells. Cover each pie with shredded cheese, almonds and Italian seasoning. Bake 20 minutes.

12 to 16 servings

Otto Walta and Ole Varmlanning are two folk heroes who arose from the working people of the early settlements. Otto was a bigger-than-life Finnish immigrant who lived near Virginia in the early 1900's. His popularity was due to his extraordinary feats of strength and courage. Ole, on the other hand, had a different appeal. A big, strong, easy-going working class Swede with an aversion to work, his good-natured jokes made tales of him full of fun.

Heroic Sirloin Tip

1 (3-pound) sirloin tip
  steak
1 medium onion, chopped
1 medium green or red
  bell pepper, chopped
5 tablespoons butter or
  margarine
3 tablespoons flour
3 cups cream
  Worcestershire sauce
  Salt

Cut steak into 1-inch wide strips. Sauté onion and pepper in 2 tablespoons butter until onion just becomes translucent; set aside. Fry steak to desired doneness; set aside but keep warm. In medium saucepan, slowly melt remaining 3 tablespoons butter. Remove from heat and add flour, stirring until smooth. Slowly add cream, stirring constantly. Return to heat and bring to boil, stirring constantly. Reduce heat and simmer 1 minute. Add vegetables to sauce and heat through. Add Worcestershire sauce and salt to taste. Pour sauce over beef strips and serve.

6 to 8 servings

Note: Celery and/or fresh mushrooms can be added to or substituted for onion and bell pepper.

Minnesota grapes are faced with the challenges of winter survival, resistance to disease and a consistent good taste. Despite these hardships, four vineyards are licensed to sell wine commercially: the Alexis Bailey Vineyard near Hastings; Scenic Valley Winery near Lanesboro; Northern Vineyards Winery, with independent vineyards scattered around the state and a cooperative winery and tasting room in Stillwater; and the newest addition, Chateau Devenois in Rice, opened in 1989. Based on the philosophy that the best wines come from stressed grapes, they unquestionably develop character in Minnesota, "where grapes can suffer."

Roast Beef with Shallots and Wine Sauce
"try one of our Minnesota wines"

1 (2 to 3-pound) beef tenderloin
1 tablespoon olive oil
½ teaspoon salt
½ teaspoon freshly ground black pepper
Sauce:
½ cup chopped shallots
1 tablespoon red wine vinegar
¼ cup dry red Bordeaux wine
¼ cup unsalted butter, cut into thin slices
¼ teaspoon salt

Heat oven to 450°. Rub roast all over with olive oil; sprinkle with salt and pepper. Place meat in a very shallow baking dish or pan. Roast 30 to 45 minutes. Let the roast rest for 15 to 20 minutes before slicing. For the sauce, in a small skillet, combine shallots, wine vinegar and wine. Over medium heat, bring the mixture to a boil and cook until reduced by half. Reduce heat to low; whisk in butter, slice by slice. Stir in salt. Drizzle sauce over sliced roast.

6 to 8 servings

A perenially popular topic of discussion is small town life, its relative virtues and, on the other hand, limitations. Heated controversy surrounded the subject when Sinclair "Red" Lewis published his famous novel, *Main Street.* His hometown of Sauk Centre was scandalized by his portrayal of it under the thinly-disguised pseudonym of "Gopher Prairie," but the town has since forgiven him and pays hearty tribute to its native son with the well-kept Sinclair Lewis Home and Interpretive Center. In 1930 he was the first American ever to receive the Nobel Prize for Literature and his novels are on required reading lists in high schools everywhere.

Main Street Main Dish
"Nobel prize pot roast"

1 (3½ to 4-pound) beef
blade pot roast
Flour
Vegetable oil
Salt and pepper
2 cups sliced onion
¼ cup water
¼ cup catsup
⅓ cup dry sherry
1 clove garlic, minced
¼ teaspoon dry mustard
¼ teaspoon dried
marjoram
¼ teaspoon dried
rosemary
¼ teaspoon dried thyme
1 medium bay leaf
1 (8-ounce) can sliced
mushrooms, drained
2 tablespoons flour
2 to 3 cups water

Trim excess fat from meat. Dredge meat in a little flour. In large skillet, brown meat on both sides in a little oil. Sprinkle generously with salt and pepper; add onion. Stir ¼ cup water, catsup, sherry, garlic and seasonings together; add to skillet. Add mushrooms. Cook, covered, over low heat or bake at 325° for 2 hours. Remove meat to serving platter. Discard bay leaf. Sprinkle 2 tablespoons flour into drippings in skillet; cook and stir until mixture thickens. Boil and stir 1 minute. Gradually add water until gravy is desired consistency.

6 to 8 servings

The University of Minnesota spills its domain across the Mississippi River onto what is affectionately known as the West Bank. More than just academic structures, the West Bank is an exciting cultural area of Minneapolis. In the 1960's, it fused its many student activities and mainstream culture with a very prominent and colorful counter-culture movement. Today you are likely to find Yuppies liberally mixing in with the vestiges of the Hippies of the 60's. A few of the original coffeehouses and bars where artists like Bob Dylan got their start are open yet, some still carrying on the tradition of showcasing new talent. The West Bank was also an historic Scandinavian area known as Snoose Boulevard.

West Bank Flank Steak
"with pistachio stuffing"

2 pounds flank steak
½ large onion, chopped
1 clove garlic, minced
2 tablespoons butter
½ cup chopped fresh mushrooms
¼ cup coarsely chopped pistachio nuts
¼ cup chopped parsley
1½ cups soft bread cubes
¾ teaspoon poultry seasoning
½ teaspoon salt
Pepper to taste
1 egg, slightly beaten
Vegetable oil
½ cup water, bouillon or dry wine

Pound flank steak. In skillet, sauté onion and garlic in butter until lightly browned. Stir in mushrooms; cook 3 minutes. Add nuts, parsley, bread cubes, seasonings and egg; mix well. Spread mixture on steak; roll lengthwise as for jelly roll, and tie with string at 2-inch intervals. In a large skillet or Dutch oven, brown meat on both sides in a little oil. Add liquid; cover and bake at 350° for 2 hours. Cut into 1-inch slices and serve with pan juices.

4 to 5 servings

A Minnesota buffalo in New York City? Ja, sure. State legislators sent him as a delegate to the Capital Palace Exhibition in 1853. Accompanied by a birch bark canoe and a Red River ox-cart, he represented our state in some of the first advertising done to bring in settlers. This coincided with the efforts of James Goodhue, editor of the first Minnesota newspaper, started in St. Paul in 1849. He was a great promoter of both settlement and tourism with his glowing journalism describing our beautiful scenery, healthful climate, fertile soil and economic opportunities. Some things haven't changed.

Delmonico Steaks
"great for backyard grilling"

4 **beef round or chuck steaks (2 inches thick)**
Instant meat tenderizer
Marinade:
2 **packages Good Seasons Italian dressing mix**
½ **cup soy sauce**
1 **cup catsup**
2 **tablespoons vegetable oil**
1 **tablespoon pepper**

Sprinkle both sides of meat with tenderizer and pierce all over with fork. Mix marinade; pour over meat and pierce again with fork. Marinate meat in refrigerator for at least 8 hours, turning and piercing it periodically. Grill 10 minutes per side for rare to medium, 12 to 15 minutes per side for medium to well-done.

4 servings

The "boss" or hump of the buffalo was considered to be the prime eating delicacy of the beast. A feminine connoisseur of buffalo compared it to a tenderloin because of the strip of lean and the strip of fat. (This same woman considered a deboned dried beaver's tail wonderful.) The last wild buffalo was seen in 1868 headed for North Dakota with a bullet in its side.

Beef Stroganoff
"real boss"

2 pounds round steak or stewing beef, cut up
1 cup wine or water
2 (10¾-ounce) cans golden mushroom soup
1 (8-ounce) can mushrooms, drained
1 envelope dry onion soup mix
  Hot cooked rice or noodles
  Dairy sour cream, optional

Mix all ingredients except rice and sour cream in casserole or crockpot. Bake at 325° for about 3 hours or cook in crockpot on low 6 to 8 hours. Serve over rice or noodles. Top with sour cream.

6 to 8 servings

Onions on your bananas? Coconut on your green pepper? Peanuts on your tomatoes? No, it's not a joke. In countries of the Middle East where curry is king, it's a sign of wealth to have a wide variety of condiments to sprinkle on top — the more the merrier. Known fondly as an "Anna Purna" dinner, this concept carried to its Minnesota extreme can become an exotic adventure in the combination of tastes and textures. Dozens of creative additions are possible. Try: bacon bits, hard-boiled egg, peas, cashews, mandarin oranges, olives, cheese, carrots, cucumber, chutney, etc., etc. The truly fearless have been known to go as far as chocolate chips and marshmallows, but this is a rather reckless departure from the traditional.

Beef Curry — Tanzanian Style
"get daring"

½ cup minced onion
¼ cup butter
2 to 3 tablespoons curry powder
¼ cup flour
2¼ cups boiling milk
4 to 6 tablespoons whipping cream
Salt and pepper to taste
Lemon juice to taste
1 pound cubed beef
1 to 2 tablespoons butter, softened
Hot cooked rice
Condiments:
Chopped onion
Chopped peanuts
Chopped green pepper
Chopped banana
Chopped apple
Chopped tomato
Raisins
Shredded coconut

Cook onion in butter over low heat 10 minutes; do not brown. Gradually stir in curry powder; cook slowly 2 minutes. Add flour and stir over low heat 3 minutes. Remove from heat and blend in boiling milk. Return to heat and simmer slowly 10 to 15 minutes, stirring occasionally. Stir in whipping cream, 1 tablespoon at a time, until sauce is desired consistency. Add salt, pepper and lemon juice. Brown beef, cook over low until done. Add to sauce. Remove from heat and gradually add butter, just before serving. Arrange rice, Curry Sauce and condiments buffet style.

4 to 6 servings

Hubert H. Humphrey has been called Minnesota's favorite son. Starting as mayor of Minneapolis, he went on to become Vice President of the United States. In 1968, he won the Democratic candidacy for president over another Minnesotan, Eugene McCarthy, but lost the office to Richard Nixon. Minnesotan Walter Mondale became Vice President of the United States under Carter in 1976, and although he lost a presidential bid in 1984, he will go down in history as having the first woman running mate, Geraldine Ferraro.

Political Barbeque
"a beefy candidate"

1 (3½ to 4-pound) beef chuck roast
½ cup vinegar
1 (28-ounce) bottle catsup
2 tablespoons Worcestershire sauce
3 bay leaves
1 large onion, chopped
1 cup water
¼ cup sugar

Combine all ingredients except sugar in large kettle or Dutch oven. Heat to boiling, reduce heat and simmer 4 to 5 hours until meat is tender and breaks apart easily. Break up meat. Refrigerate overnight. Skim off fat. Add sugar and reheat. Discard bay leaves before serving on warm hamburger buns.

12 to 14 servings

Allemande left and Promenade! It's easy to find a place to kick up your heels in Minnesota, blessed with public ballrooms from border to border. The Twin Cities alone has more than 10% of the total public ballrooms in the country. Add to that all the folk, ethnic and square dancing clubs, the live band and disco bars, and the sum is one swinging, swaying, spinning state of motion. Dance of various forms is the theme for many festivals, too. Gibbon's Polka Fest brings dancers from all over the country. It's no wonder that this is called the "Ballroom Capital of the United States."

Wild Rice Meatballs

1 pound ground beef
1 small onion, finely chopped
½ cup cooked wild rice
½ teaspoon seasoned salt
½ teaspoon garlic salt
⅓ cup fine dry bread crumbs
½ cup evaporated milk
1 (10¾-ounce) can cream of mushroom soup
⅔ cup water
⅔ cup dry white wine
¼ teaspoon dried sage
½ teaspoon salt
  Pepper to taste

Heat oven to 375°. Combine beef, onion, rice, salts, bread crumbs and milk; shape into 1-inch balls. Place in shallow pan; bake 10 to 15 minutes or until brown. In saucepan, combine soup, water, wine and spices. Add meatballs and simmer 30 minutes.

4 servings

Alexandria and Detroit Lakes mark the corners of the Lake Region. Splashed with hundreds of sparkling lakes, this area draws multitudes of tourists for fishing, swimming, boating, ice fishing and snowmobiling. Detroit Lakes' summer country music festival is growing in popularity and Alexandria continually draws curious visitors to see the controversial Kensington Runestone. There the world's largest Viking, Big Ole, presides over the comings and goings of vacationers and residents along the main street.

Lake Region Meatballs

1½ pounds ground beef
12 ounces pork sausage
 2 medium potatoes,
    boiled and mashed
 2 eggs
 1 medium onion, chopped
 2 tablespoons allspice
 1 teaspoon salt
 1 teaspoon pepper
    Flour
 ¼ teaspoon salt
 6 strips bacon

Combine meat, potatoes, eggs, onion, and seasonings; shape into small meatballs. Roll in flour. Heat a large saucepan of water to boiling; add salt. Cook about 20 meatballs at a time, for 10 minutes. Line a large skillet with bacon; place boiled meatballs on bacon in pan. Fry bacon and meatballs until bacon is done. Serve meatballs.

Makes about 80 meatballs

The empyreal World Trade Center soaring up from St. Paul's skyline is like a highly visible arrow pointing out our state's commitment to international commerce, long since established by such institutions as the Minneapolis Grain Exchange, the South St. Paul stockyards and Great Lakes shipping. But on a blustery June day in 1990 the eyes of the world turned our way like never before when Mikhail Gorbachev and his wife Raisa visited the Twin Cities as part of Governor Rudy Perpich's promotion of direct trade links between Minnesota and the U.S.S.R. Hundreds of thousands of people lined the streets of Minneapolis and St. Paul to greet the Gorbachevs, who repeatedly stopped their motorcade to venture into the crowds and shake hands. Their busy afternoon also included touring two stores and addressing an assembly of business leaders. All this Russian around gave them just enough time to meet, but not loaf.

Italian Meat Loaf
"a good international trade"

Meat loaf:
½ cup cracker crumbs
1½ pounds ground beef
1 (12-ounce) can tomato paste
½ cup chopped onion
2 eggs
¼ cup chopped green pepper
¾ teaspoon salt
Dash of pepper
Filling:
½ cup cracker crumbs
1 (12-ounce) carton cottage cheese
1 (4-ounce) can mushroom stems and pieces, drained
1 tablespoon snipped fresh parsley
¼ teaspoon dried oregano

Combine meat loaf ingredients; pat half of mixture into 8x8x2-inch pan. Combine filling ingredients; spread evenly over meat. Spread remaining meat mixture over filling. Bake at 350° for 1 hour. Let stand 10 minutes.

9 servings

"Reformatory Pink" is the fashionably cryptic name given to the lovely rosy hue that comes from the granite quarries around St. Cloud, where the state reformatory is now located. This imposing hard stone is often used for monuments, gravestones and other cryptic applications.

Lasagne
"as Italian as Rocky"

1 pound lasagne noodles
1 teaspoon olive oil
1 pound ricotta cheese
1 egg
1 pound Mozzarella cheese, shredded
1 cup grated Parmesan cheese
Sauce:
1 cup chopped onion
1 clove garlic, minced
2 tablespoons olive oil
1½ pounds ground beef
2 teaspoons salt
1 (28-ounce) can tomatoes
1 (8-ounce) can tomato sauce
1 (6-ounce) can tomato paste
½ cup water
½ teaspoon dried basil
½ teaspoon dried oregano
1 teaspoon sugar
1 tablespoon dried parsley flakes

To prepare sauce, sauté onion and garlic in olive oil 5 minutes. Add ground beef and brown; drain off fat. Stir in remaining sauce ingredients; heat to boiling, reduce heat and simmer 45 minutes. Cook noodles according to package directions; add olive oil to prevent sticking. Drain, rinse and cool. Blend ricotta cheese and egg together. Heat oven to 350°. Grease 13x9x2-inch pan. Layer ⅓ of sauce, half of noodles, half of ricotta cheese and half of Mozzarella cheese in pan. Repeat layers, ending with sauce. Sprinkle with Parmesan cheese. Bake 35 minutes; let stand 10 minutes before serving.

8 to 10 servings

The Ojibwe (Chippewa) and the Dakota (Sioux) fought over Minnesota land, particularly the spiritual center of Lake Mille Lacs. One of their encounters is graphically portrayed by an interesting effigy mound near Lake Winnibigoshish. When the Sioux defeated the Chippewa, they built a 30-foot long turtle mound to mark the victory. The head of the turtle points north, showing the direction in which the Chippewa fled. When the Chippewa retaliated and reclaimed the territory, they built a snake around the turtle, proving their superiority. The head and tail of the snake pointed south, the direction in which they continued to push the Sioux.

Wild Rice-Ground Beef Casserole

4 cups boiling water
1 cup uncooked wild rice
1 (10¾-ounce) can cream of mushroom soup
1 (10¾-ounce) can cream of chicken or cream of celery soup
1 (8-ounce) can sliced mushrooms, drained, or 1 pound fresh mushrooms
2 beef bouillon cubes dissolved in 1 cup boiling water or 1 (10½-ounce) can beef broth
1 bay leaf, crumbled
¼ teaspoon celery salt
¼ teaspoon garlic salt
¼ teaspoon pepper
¼ teaspoon onion salt
¼ teaspoon paprika
½ to ¾ cup chopped celery
½ cup chopped onion
3 tablespoon butter
1½ to 2 pounds ground beef
½ cup slivered almonds

Pour boiling water over rice and let stand 15 minutes; drain. Add soups, mushrooms, bouillon cubes, bay leaf and spices. Sauté celery and onion in butter until transparent; add to rice mixture. Brown ground beef; drain off fat. Add beef to rice mixture; place in casserole and sprinkle with almonds. Bake at 350° for 1½ hours. Add more broth or water if it becomes dry during baking.

8 servings

Once upon a time, long ago, four huge sheets of glacial ice moved slowly across Minnesota, leaving their eternal impression on our topography, flattening the land and creating more than 10,000 lakes. The Driftless area south of Winona was untouched by actual glaciers, but as the ice melted in the north the glacial waters rushed through, tearing and ripping at the land. Valleys and coulees were gouged out, and a fine silt was deposited over the limestone hills. This created some of the most fertile farmland in the world, perfect for dairy farming, wheat, apples, and a wide variety of trees.

Four Sheet Dinner
"great for your Minnesota-grown vegetables"

1½ pounds ground beef
1 cup sliced onion
2 cups sliced carrot
4 cups sliced potato
2 (10¾-ounce) cans cream
   of mushroom soup
1⅓ cups milk
Salt and pepper to taste

Brown ground beef; drain. Place in 13x9x2-inch casserole. Layer onion, carrot and potato over meat. Combine soup, milk, salt and pepper; pour over vegetables. Cover with aluminum foil. Bake at 350° for 1½ hours.

6 to 8 servings

Mendota, just across the Mississippi River from Fort Snelling, is the oldest continuous settlement in Minnesota. After the Indian treaties were signed in the 1850's and the military lands were opened, settlers flooded in to homestead. Following a series of disasters, many of these early settlers grew disheartened and left. But they were replaced by a persistent new flood of immigrants in the 1880's, bringing new determination as well as an ever-broadening cultural and ethnic scope to our state.

Unsinkable Sauerkraut
"a staunch hot dish"

1½ pounds ground beef
1 medium onion, chopped
1 (16-ounce) can sauerkraut
1 (8-ounce) package wide noodles, cooked and drained
1 (10¾-ounce) can cream of chicken soup
Salt and pepper to taste

Brown ground beef and onion; drain. Combine with undrained sauerkraut and remaining ingredients. Bake at 350° for 1¼ hours.

6 servings

Norwegian pioneers imported skiing to Minnesota, and they organized the first ski club in Red Wing in the 1880's. Alpine skiing now enjoys great popularity, served by over 35 ski areas around the state.

Norwegian Liver with Apple

2 large onions, sliced
1 medium green pepper, seeded and sliced
1 apple, peeled, cored and cut into chunks
3 tablespoons margarine
½ cup beef bouillon
1½ teaspoons Worcestershire sauce
1 pound beef or calf liver Salt and pepper
2 tablespoons margarine

Sauté onions, green pepper and apple in margarine until soft; stir in bouillon and Worcestershire sauce. Keep sauce warm. Cut liver into serving-size pieces; sprinkle with salt and pepper. Fry in margarine over very low heat until done. Add liver to sauce and heat together a few minutes. Thicken the sauce with 1 teaspoon cornstarch, dissolved in a little water, if desired. Excellent served with mashed potatoes.

5 to 6 servings

Venison Roast — German Style

1 (3½-pound) venison roast
½ pound bacon
Salt
White pepper
Margarine
1 cup cream
Marinade:
3 cups salted water
2 carrots, cubed
2 onions, chopped
6 juniper berries
1 bay leaf
1 teaspoon dried thyme
1 teaspoon dried marjoram
8 whole peppercorns
3 cups buttermilk
5 cups red wine

To prepare marinade, cook carrots and onions in water 25 minutes. Add remaining marinade ingredients; heat to boiling, reduce heat and simmer a few minutes. Cool. Rinse and dry roast. Remove any remaining thin-skin. Put roast in a large bowl and completely cover with marinade. Cover and refrigerate 2 days, turning meat occasionally.

Remove meat from marinade and dry. Reserve the vegetables and 1 cup of the marinade. Cut bacon into small strips; freeze about 30 minutes. Remove bacon from freezer and pin to roast with larding pins. Season roast with salt and pepper. Heat margarine in large kettle or Dutch oven and brown meat on all sides. Add reserved vegetables and brown 5 minutes longer. Cover kettle and place on middle rack in oven. Bake at 350° for 2 hours, basting meat frequently with its own juice. When meat begins to pull away from bone, reduce oven temperature to 300°. When meat is done, remove roast from oven, slice and keep warm. To make gravy, loosen drippings in pan by adding reserved marinade and heating to a boil. Strain drippings; add cream and season with salt and pepper. Serve meat and gravy separately. Serve with Red Cabbage, page 141.

5 to 6 servings

Hint: Roast can also be prepared in an oven-roasting bag. Place vegetables and roast in bag and follow bag package directions for roasting. When roast is done, drain juices into saucepan and prepare gravy as above.

In an area that is notably unforested, it is interesting that the town of Winona is supported, both above and below, indirectly by trees. The town was built upon thousands of tons of sawdust, laid down to reinforce the treeless sand plain; also the town's numerous millionaires (more than any other town of its size) made their fortunes on lumber and sawmills. A Mississippi River town landmarked by the huge Sugarloaf Mountain, Winona was once a major steamboat and trade center. Winona has the distinction of once being the largest sauerkraut producer west of Chicago. They still enjoy their kraut, and there is no better way than this:

Sauerkraut and Pork with Spatzen

1 (3 to 4-pound) boneless
   pork roast
   Salt and pepper
2 to 3 cloves garlic,
   minced
1 teaspoon poultry
   seasoning
1 quart sauerkraut
1 medium onion, diced
2 to 3 apples, shredded
¼ teaspoon nutmeg
2 tablespoons brown
   sugar
2 tablespoons molasses
   Spatzen (per serving):
1 egg
2 tablespoons water
   Salt and pepper to taste
   Garlic to taste
   Sugar to taste
3 to 4 teaspoons flour

Season pork well with salt, pepper, garlic and poultry seasoning. Brown roast in large kettle or Dutch oven; add remaining ingredients. Add enough water to cover roast; simmer 2 hours. Beat spatzen ingredients together; drop by teaspoonful into sauerkraut mixture and steam 20 minutes. Potato pieces could also be added at this time.

6 to 8 servings

The Norway pine or "red pine" is distinguished by its tall, straight reddish-brown trunk with branches only on the top half. Valuable for its lumber, this tree suffered heavy casualties during the logging days, but it was named our state tree in 1953 and is slowly being replenished. A six-foot Norway pine took flight in October, 1984, when it was flown from Pillsbury State Forest to Washington, D.C. to embrace roots with state trees from 33 other states on the capitol grounds.

Peachy Minnesota Pork Roast
"a stately dish"

1 (3 to 4-pound) pork
  roast
1 (16-ounce) can sliced
  peaches
¼ cup catsup
2 teaspoons lemon juice
1 tablespoon cornstarch
2 tablespoons sugar
¼ teaspoon cinnamon
⅛ teaspoon ground cloves
¼ teaspoon salt
½ cup cream
¼ cup brandy, optional

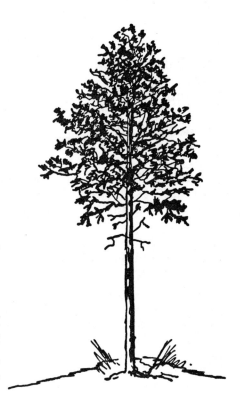

Place pork roast in roasting pan. Bake at 325° for about 3 hours, until internal temperature is 170°. Just before serving, prepare sauce: drain peaches, reserving juice. Combine peach juice, catsup and lemon juice. Mix cornstarch, sugar, cinnamon, ground cloves and salt. Stir in peach juice mixture. Cook over medium heat, stirring constantly, until thickened. Add cream and brandy; heat. Add peach slices. Serve as accompaniment to roast.

6 to 8 servings

Explore Minnesota! is the invitation extended by the Department of Tourism. And Minnesota has lots of great outdoors to explore. One of the finest in the country, our park system celebrated its 100th birthday in 1991. The DNR maintains over 60 state parks, 25 of which feature interpretive centers to inform visitors about the history, wildlife and geography of the area. We have 55 state forests that encompass more than 3 million acres, and our approximately 900 state-owned wildlife areas cover another million acres, providing nesting and feeding places for many wildlife varieties. And it's all at our toe-tips via some 1,235 miles of scenic recreational trails. Are you ready, boots? Start walking!

Stir-fry Wild Rice, Snow Peas and Pork
"explore good eating"

3 tablespoons vegetable oil
½ pound pork tenderloin, sliced ¼-inch thick
1 cup sliced celery
1 cup sliced green onion
1 cup sliced fresh mushrooms
1 (8-ounce) can sliced water chestnuts, drained
½ pound snow peas or edible-pod peas, fresh or frozen, thawed
1 tablespoon grated fresh ginger root
2 cups cooked wild rice
1 tablespoon cornstarch
1 tablespoon dry sherry
3 tablespoons soy sauce
½ teaspoon salt
½ cup cashews or sunflower nuts
Shredded carrot or carrot cut-outs

Heat oil in heavy skillet; add pork and stir-fry over high heat for 2 minutes until meat is no longer pink. Add celery, green onion, mushrooms, water chestnuts, pea pods and ginger. Stir-fry for 5 minutes over high heat until vegetables are tender-crisp. Toss in wild rice until evenly blended. Mix cornstarch with sherry, soy sauce and salt; add to juices in pan and cook about 1 minute until thickened. Toss mixture together to coat evenly with glaze. Garnish with nuts and carrots.

4 servings

No longer limited to New York Mills and Embarrass, Finnish steam baths are a ritual of some refinement, magically mingling thick steam with the cleansing oils of cedar wood within the walls of their small, intimate enclosures. A custom brought from Finland in about 1883, it was a tradition initially misunderstood by outsiders, who assessed it to be some bizarre form of "Devil Worship," with people strangely wrapped in white, dashing in a cloud of steam into the cold lakes. Now the sauna is a popular and healthy pastime for all nationalities.

Kerelian Steak
"you'll finish every bite"

1 pound pork
⅔ pound beef
½ pound lamb
1 tablespoon salt
2 onions, sliced
10 whole allspice
10 whole white
    peppercorns

Cut meat into cubes and place in casserole. Sprinkle with salt; add onions, allspice, pepper and enough water to cover meat. Bake at 350° for 2 hours.

6 to 8 servings

St. Urho

117

Grand Portage was the first white settlement in Minnesota, started in 1731 as a fur-trading post. It was the "Rendezvous" point for the highly-romanticized Voyageurs. The "Winterers" came from the wilderness of the Northwest Territory loaded with furs and pelts. They portaged the last 8½ miles of their journey to avoid the treacherous falls of the Pigeon River, hence the name "Grand Portage." Each voyageur was loaded with about 180 pounds, and they managed the distance in about 2½ hours. A second group, known as "Pork Eaters" because they spent their winters in relative comfort in Montreal, came across Lake Superior in 36-foot canoes loaded with up to 4 tons of supplies to meet the "Winterers" and exchange cargoes. The "Rendezvous," which took place in July, was marked by much revelry. The reconstructed trading post is now a National Monument, attracting tourists from the world over with its scenic beauty and colorful, unique history.

Grilled Pork
"Pork Eater's delight"

¼ cup soy sauce
2 tablespoons dry red wine
1 tablespoon brown sugar
1 tablespoon honey
2 teapoons red food coloring, optional
½ teaspoon cinnamon
1 clove garlic, crushed
1 green onion, cut into pieces
1 (2-pound) pork tenderloin

Combine all ingredients except pork in large bowl. Place pork in bowl; cover and let stand at room temperature 1 hour or in refrigerator ovenight, turning occasionally. Drain and grill pork.

6 to 8 servings

The first white settler in St. Paul was "Pig's Eye" Parrant, who staked his claim in 1837 at the foot of the present-day Robert Street Bridge. He was, by all accounts, a "sinister-looking scoundrel" and a "vagrant voyageur" who sold liquor illegally to Indians and Ft. Snelling soldiers. The city was originally called "Pig's Eye," but the influence of the church changed it to St. Paul.

Pork on the Rocks

1 cup soy sauce
1 cup packed brown sugar
1 cup bourbon
¾ to 1-inch thick pork chops

Mix soy sauce, brown sugar and bourbon; marinate pork chops in sauce 4 to 6 hours or overnight. Grill chops in Weber kettle about 30 minutes, basting often. Remaining marinade can be stored in a covered jar in refrigerator; before using, shake well and add a little more bourbon.

Makes about 2½ cups

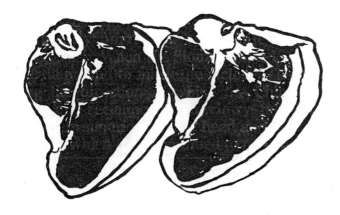

The Mesabi Iron Range is the best-known iron-producing region of Minnesota, not only because it had the largest concentration of ore, but because it boasts the largest open pit mine in the world—over 3 miles long and a mile wide. The Hull-Rust-Mahoning Mine in Hibbing incorporates what was once 50 individual mines. Other noteworthy features of the Mesabi Range are the "Quad Cities" of Virginia, Eveleth, Gilbert and Mountain Iron, and the comprehensive Minnesota Museum of Mining and the Iron Range Interpretive Center in Chisholm.

Home on the Range Barbeque

8 to 10 pounds country-style or regular spareribs
Lemon slices
Sauce:
2½ teaspoons celery salt
2 teaspoons paprika
7 to 10 tablespoons sugar
2 tablespoons grated onion
2½ teaspoons garlic salt
2½ teaspoons dry mustard
1¼ teaspoon black pepper
10 tablespoons Worcestershire sauce
2 cups cold water
1¼ cups catsup
10 tablespoons white vinegar

Bake spareribs at 350° for 1 hour; drain off fat. Meanwhile, combine all sauce ingredients in saucepan. Simmer until well blended. Place lemon slice on each section of ribs. Baste with sauce. Bake 1 hour longer, basting with sauce every 10 minutes.

8 to 10 servings

When iron mining began in Minnesota in the late 1890's, there was much conflict between the miners and the loggers since they were in competition for the same lands. As the trees vanished from the mining region, so did the lumbermen. "Da Range" is the mixing bowl of Minnesota, commingling descendants of 43 different nations, many of them Slavic and Finnish. This diversity is one reason that Range towns and residents have their own particular style unlike the rest of Minnesota. Although the widely varied cultures and traditions have been closely interwoven, they have not been homogenized, and each has retained its own essence. Today, the Rangers take great pride in their rich and varied ethnic heritage.

Halupke

1 large or 2 small heads cabbage
½ cup uncooked rice
2½ pounds ground shoulder pork
1 egg
2 teaspoons salt
Pepper to taste
1 (2½-pound) can sauerkraut
1 (8-ounce) can tomato sauce
2 cups dairy sour cream

Core cabbage; cook in boiling water a few minutes until leaves are soft and can easily be separated. Cut off heavy membrane. Cook rice 2 minutes; drain and add to pork. Add egg, salt and pepper; mix well. Place large tablespoon of filling on each leaf and roll up, tucking in the ends. Layer the rolls in a large kettle. Cover rolls with sauerkraut; pour tomato sauce over all. Cook, covered, over low heat 1½ to 2 hours. Serve topped with sour cream.

Makes about 24 rolls

The Landmark Center in St. Paul was the old Federal Courts Building. Its walls witnessed the famous gangster trials of the 1930's. Situated next to Rice Park, a pretty setting for art fairs in the summer and ice sculpture in the winter, the handsomely renovated Landmark Center now houses numerous cultural groups.

Wild Rice-Sausage Casserole
"a Minnesota landmark"

1 pound smoked sausage
1 cup finely chopped celery
½ cup finely chopped onion
½ cup finely chopped green pepper
1 cup uncooked wild rice
½ cup blanched almonds
1 (4-ounce) can mushrooms
1 (8-ounce) can sliced water chestnuts, drained
4½ cups water
2 envelopes dry chicken noodle soup mix with diced chicken
½ cup cooking sherry
Fried onion rings, browned, optional

Brown sausage; remove from pan and cut diagonally into 1-inch pieces. In sausage drippings, sauté celery, onion and green pepper. In large bowl, put meat, sautéed vegetables, rice, almonds, mushrooms and water chestnuts. In saucepan, bring water to a boil and add soup mix. Return to boiling and add other ingredients. Mix and pour all into greased casserole. Let stand at least 10 hours or overnight. Bake, covered, at 325° for 1½ hours. Remove from oven and pour sherry over top of casserole. Return to oven for a few minutes. Add onion rings to top before serving.

4 to 6 servings

Ham Roll with Horseradish Sauce

Crust:
1½ to 2 cups all-purpose flour
½ teaspoon baking soda
¼ teaspoon salt
2 teaspoons baking powder
¼ cup butter
⅔ cup buttermilk
Melted butter
Filling:
2½ to 3 cups ground ham
½ teaspoon dry mustard
¼ cup minced onion
¼ cup chopped green pepper
⅓ cup buttermilk
Milk

Heat oven to 375°. To make crust, mix dry ingredients together. Cut in butter; stir in buttermilk. Knead lightly, adding flour, if necessary. Roll pastry crust out to a rectangle about 12x7 inches. Brush with melted butter. Combine ham, mustard, onion, green pepper and buttermilk; spread on pastry. Roll as for jelly roll; brush with milk. Place on ungreased cookie sheet. Bake 30 to 40 minutes. Cool 5 minutes; slice and serve with Horseradish Sauce.

4 to 5 servings

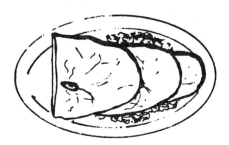

Horseradish Sauce

¼ cup butter
¼ cup flour
½ teaspoon salt
⅛ teaspoon pepper
2 cups milk
½ to 1 teaspoon cornstarch, optional
2 tablespoons drained prepared horseradish

Melt butter in saucepan over low heat. Blend in flour, salt and pepper. Cook over low heat, stirring constantly, until smooth and bubbly. Remove from heat. Stir in milk and heat to boiling, stirring constantly. Boil and stir 1 minute. Thicken sauce with cornstarch, if desired. Stir in horseradish. Serve with Ham Loaf.

Makes about 2½ cups

Duluth, nestled on the southeastern corner of Lake Superior, has an impressive list of credits to recommend it for visiting or habitation. The tonnage shipped through this international port is second only to New York City. One of two aerial bridges in the world graces its charming harbor skyline, which at night looks like a string of pearls. It is a culturally active city which takes pride in its heritage. It is the home of the Ice Capades, Grandma's Marathon and a large branch of the University of Minnesota. If you suffer from pollinosis, you might find solace in Duluth, distinguished center of the Hayfever Club of America. This city is nothing to sneeze at!

Fish with Sour Cream

1½ pounds fish fillets
1 cup dairy sour cream
1½ teaspoons Beau Monde seasoning
1 tablespoon soy sauce
¼ teaspoon horseradish
1 tablespoon minced chives
Paprika

Place fish in shallow baking dish. Combine remaining ingredients; spread over fish. Bake at 400° for 25 to 30 minutes.

5 to 6 servings

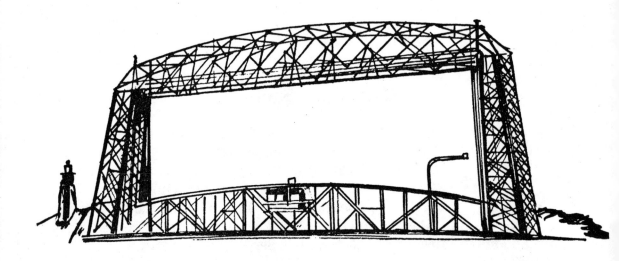

Minnesota = Fishing: a well-known equation among sportsmen. And we wouldn't expect otherwise from a state which boasts more than 25,000 miles of rivers and streams and over 12,000 lakes. There are 144 species of fish to hook, but Minnesota is most known for walleye, northerns, muskie, bass, pan fish, trout and smelt. King Walleye, the old "Marble Eye," is our state fish. One out of every three people in Minnesota has a fishing license and, although 90 percent of the fish are caught by 10 percent of the fishermen, the other 90 percent of us can have fun trying.

Baked Walleye
"100% delectable"

2 **walleye fillets**
Salt and pepper
Lemon juice
Sliced colby or Cheddar cheese
Grated onion
Cheese Sauce:
2 **tablespoons butter**
2 **tablespoons flour**
¼ **teaspoon salt**
⅛ **teaspoon pepper**
1 **cup milk**
Cubed Velveeta or American cheese

Place one fish fillet in greased 13x9x2-inch pan. Sprinkle with salt, pepper and lemon juice. Layer with sliced cheese and sprinkle with onion. Cover with second fillet. Sprinkle with salt, pepper and lemon juice. To make cheese sauce, melt butter in small saucepan, stir in flour, salt and pepper. Gradually stir in milk; cook, stirring constantly until mixture thickens and boils. Boil and stir 1 minute. Add cheese to taste. Pour cheese sauce over fillets. Bake, uncovered, at 350° for 30 to 45 minutes until sauce is bubbly.

2 servings

Water skiing was invented by an enterprising 18-year-old named Ralph S. Samuelson in 1922. Using two curved boards that cost him $1 each, he executed his daring exploit on Lake Pepin with a minimum of floundering.

No-Flop Flounder

2 (10-ounce) packages
   frozen spinach, thawed
   and drained
1 cup diary sour cream
1 tablespoon flour
½ teaspoon salt
¼ teaspoon nutmeg
   Dash of pepper
1 pound flounder or
   orange roughy
2 tablespoons butter
¼ teaspoon salt
1½ teaspoons paprika
⅓ cup shredded Swiss
   cheese

Combine spinach with sour cream, flour, salt, nutmeg and pepper; mix well. Spoon into shallow greased casserole or baking dish. Rinse fish; dry with paper towel. Place fish on top of spinach mixture in a single layer. Melt butter; brush on fish. Sprinkle fish with salt, paprika and cheese. Bake at 375° for 30 minutes.

3 to 4 servings

The Muskie Rampage is a fish story that won't be topped. In a period of two days in 1955, fishermen on Leech Lake caught 51 muskies weighing between 18 and 41 pounds each. At an average weight of 23 pounds, muskies are considered a "trophy" fish, so the sport of landing one is more important than the catch. Another Leech Lake sport is pursued at the Eelpout Festival in Walker in February, when busloads of people arrive to compete in catching the most pounds of the least-prized fish, the ugly eelpout.

Fish Cakes
"a no-pout treat"

¾ cup milk
1 egg
1 tablespoon vegetable oil
1 teaspoon cornstarch
¼ to ½ small onion
¼ teaspoon mace
  Dash of pepper
2 cups herring or
  northern fillets, cut into
  1-inch pieces
1 teaspoon salt

In blender, combine milk, egg, oil, cornstarch, onion, mace and pepper. Stop blender and add fish. Blend, using short on-and-off spurts, just until fish is mixed in. Pour mixture into bowl; add salt. Cover bottom of skillet with oil and heat. Drop fish mixture into pan by teaspoonful. Fry on both sides until golden.

4 to 5 servings

Hint: Overblending will make mixture too soupy, so use caution. If mixture is too thick, add milk to thin.

The spring ritual of smelting draws thousands of people to the rivers running into Lake Superior around Duluth. The "smelt report" phone in Duluth receives up to 6400 long-distance calls each season from sportsmen waiting for word that "the run is on!" Using nets and buckets instead of rods, reels and bait to harvest the small, silvery fish on their spawning runs, the most avid fishers will spend endless hours standing in hip boots in the frigid shallow waters. Part of the ritual is the yearly reunion and swapping of fish tales with other smelters, but there are no stories of "the big one that got away." We're talking sheer numbers here. This plentitude is celebrated with smelt fries in small towns all over the state. Smelt are good pickled and smoked, but we'd recommend this recipe for your haul.

Deep-Fried Smelt
"eat all but the wiggle"

1 egg yolk, beaten
1 cup ice water
¾ cup all-purpose flour
Oil for deep-frying
Smelt

Combine egg yolk and water; beat until smooth. Add flour and stir with spoon (batter should be runny). Chill several hours. Heat oil to 350°. Dip smelt in batter (will form a thin film). Deep fry 2 to 4 minutes, until fish rise to surface. Be sure oil reheats between batches. Eat immediately!

Note: This batter can also be used for sunfish or other small fish. For larger fish (over ½ inch thick), decrease water to ½ cup and fry fish 10 to 15 minutes in lower temperature oil.

The World's Largest Outdoor Fish Fry is a highlight of the Voyageur Day Celebration in Crane Lake, once the site of a large fur-trading post. As you sit around an open campfire under the approving eye of the giant Voyageur statue, eating fresh-fried fish, you can sense the flair and flavor of another time and way of life.

Open-Fire Fish Fry
"can't have a better fish"

Onion rings
Walleye, bass, northern
or other pan fish
Batter:
3 cups biscuit mix
1 (12-ounce) can beer
1 egg, beaten
Salt and pepper

Combine batter ingredients; dip fish and onions into batter. Fry in hot oil over open fire for 1 to 2 minutes per side.

Makes about 4 cups batter

Beer Batter

1 cup plus 1 tablespoon
flour
Salt
1 tablespoon oil
¾ cup beer at room
temperature
2 tablespoons warm
water
1 egg, separated

Mix flour, salt and oil. Add beer and water, while stirring. Beat in egg yolk. Let stand, covered, in warm place 2 to 3 hours. Beat egg white until stiff; fold into batter.

Makes about 2½ cups

The button factories in Lake City buttoned up when synthetic buttons replaced mother-of-pearl, but in the early 1900's 500-600 river clammers working along the shores of Lake Pepin created a picturesque scene.

Clam Up with Linguini

1 small onion, finely chopped
2 tablespoons olive oil
8 to 10 cloves garlic, finely chopped
4 (6½-ounce) cans clams
1 tablespoon white wine
1 tablespoon lemon juice
½ teaspoon salt
1 teaspoon chopped fresh parsley
½ teaspoon dried basil (½ tablespoon chopped fresh basil)
⅛ teaspoon pepper
Dash of dried oregano
1 teaspoon cornstarch
2 tablespoons white wine
Hot linguini, cooked al dente
Grated Parmesan cheese

Sauté onion in olive oil until almost transparent. Add garlic; sauté, but do not brown. Drain clams; add juice to onion. Add 1 tablespoon wine, lemon juice, salt, parsley, basil, pepper and oregano; simmer. Mix cornstarch and remaining wine to make a paste; add to sauce, simmer until thickened. Add clams, cook just to heat through. Serve over linguini; sprinkle with Parmesan cheese.

4 servings

Staunch, sturdy and stable steamboats were once the main lifeline connecting Minnesota to the outside world, transporting freight, supplies and settlers in and out. There was a strong rivalry among the riverboat captains, and races on the St. Croix and Mississippi were a standard sight, with steamstackers puffing, whistling and sternwheeling their way stem-to-stem down their watery speedways. A banquet in St. Paul joyfully saluted the first captain to reach there each year and the earliest promise of spring always found 12 or more boats waiting impatiently at the foot of Lake Pepin for the ice to break up.

Captain's Quiche

1 (9-inch) unbaked pie shell
2 cups cream
4 eggs
¾ teaspoon salt
¼ cup shredded Swiss cheese
2 tablespoon minced green onion
3 tablespoons butter
2 (6-ounce) packages frozen crabmeat, thawed, drained and flaked
2 tablespoons dry sherry
¼ teaspoon salt
⅛ teaspoon cayenne pepper

Prepare pie shell. Heat oven to 425°. Blend cream, eggs, salt and cheese together. In medium saucepan, cook green onion in butter until tender. Add onion to creamed mixture. Add crab, sherry, salt and pepper. Pour into pie shell. Bake 15 minutes; reduce oven temperature to 325° and bake 35 minutes longer, or until knife inserted about 1 inch from edge comes out clean.

6 servings

Note: Two (7-ounce) cans tuna, drained and flaked or 2 (4½-ounce) cans shrimp, drained, can be substituted for crab.

The Hubert H. Humphrey Metrodome is home to the Minnesota Twins, Minnesota Vikings and U of M Gophers, and the venerable host of the 1992 Super Bowl Game. Replacing the popular open-air Metropolitan Stadium, this ever-controversial structure has suffered a few "fallen" moments since its original "Inflation Day" on October 2, 1981. "Tail-gaters" have gone the way of the dodo bird, regrettably supplanted by the ever-vigilant band of "dome-perchers" who brave the fiercest blizzards to fend off snowy drifts which can deflate the dome's airy shape. Our puffy souffle is blizzard-proof even without such attention and elegant enough for party fare. If you make a large enough batch, you might consider renting the Metrodome to serve it in grandiose style, for only $5,000 a day!

Inflation Day Soufflé
"crab-asparagus delight"

1 small onion, chopped
½ cup butter or margarine
½ cup flour
1 teaspoon salt
  Dash of white pepper
2½ cups milk
4 ounces Swiss cheese, shredded
½ teaspoon dry mustard
1 (6-ounce) package frozen crabmeat, thawed, drained and flaked
1 (10-ounce) package frozen asparagus, cooked and cut into 1-inch pieces
2 tablespoons dry sherry
4 eggs, separated

Note: One (7-ounce) can tuna, drained or 1 (8-ounce) can salmon, drained, can be substituted for crabmeat.

Heat oven to 350°. In large saucepan, sauté onion in butter until soft. Stir in flour, salt and pepper until mixture bubbles. Stir in 2 cups of the milk and cook, stirring constantly, until sauce thickens and bubbles. Cook and stir 1 minute. Reserve 1 cup of mixture in bowl. To remaining sauce in pan, add cheese and dry mustard. Heat and stir until cheese melts; remove from heat. Fold crab, asparagus, remaining milk and sherry into reserved sauce in bowl. Spoon into 8-cup soufflé dish or straight-sided casserole, pushing pieces of crab and asparagus against side of dish. In large mixer bowl, beat egg whites at high speed until soft peaks are formed. Beat egg yolks in medium bowl at high speed; blend in cheese mixture until smooth. Fold egg yolk mixture into egg whites until well blended. Spoon over sauce in soufflé dish. With table knife, cut a ring around soufflé mixture about 1 inch from edge of dish to create a "top hat". Bake 45 minutes or until puffed and golden brown. Serve immediately.

4 to 5 servings

Farm Land Vegetables
and Side Dishes

Olivia, the Corn Capital of Minnesota, pays husky respects to this princely golden vegetable by way of its annual Corn Days, and also with a majestic giant ear-of-corn monument in their park. The town was all ears when pop singer Olivia Newton-John stalked in to ride horseback as Grand Marshall in their 1978 Centennial parade. The only payment she requested was "fresh bread and two dozen ears of corn." You, too, can celebrate corn with these two a-maizing recipes.

Cornucopia Patties

1 (17-ounce) can cream-
    style corn
½ cup flour
2 eggs, beaten
    Salt and pepper

Mix all ingredients together and shape into patties. Fry about 15 minutes in generously greased skillet over medium-high heat (they scorch easily). Serve with butter.

4 servings

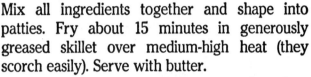

Corner on Corn Pudding

⅓ cup flour
1 (17-ounce) can cream-
    style corn
1 (17-ounce) can whole
    kernel corn
1 (3-ounce) package
    cream cheese, cubed
½ teaspoon onion salt
½ cup Swiss cheese,
    shredded
    Bread crumbs

Combine flour and corn; stir in cream cheese and onion salt. Stir in Swiss cheese. Put in 1½ to 2 quart casserole and top with bread crumbs. Bake, uncovered, at 350° for 30 to 40 minutes.

6 servings

The last 14 miles of Interstate 90, the nation's longest highway, were completed near Blue Earth in 1978. This final stretch was painted gold in color, reminiscent of the gold spike in the last tie of the Trans-Continental Railroad. The celebration was overseen by the newly arrived 50-foot Jolly Green Giant, proudly presiding over this historic juncture which would spread his peas on earth.

Peas and Cucumbers in Sour Cream

"jolly and green, a gigantic success"

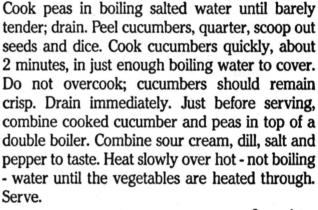

3 cups peas, fresh or frozen
2 medium cucumbers
1 cup dairy sour cream (at room temperature)
3 tablespoons finely chopped dill
Salt and pepper

Cook peas in boiling salted water until barely tender; drain. Peel cucumbers, quarter, scoop out seeds and dice. Cook cucumbers quickly, about 2 minutes, in just enough boiling water to cover. Do not overcook; cucumbers should remain crisp. Drain immediately. Just before serving, combine cooked cucumber and peas in top of a double boiler. Combine sour cream, dill, salt and pepper to taste. Heat slowly over hot - not boiling - water until the vegetables are heated through. Serve.

6 servings

Minnesota as a state has challenged the "Frontier Mentality" which supposed that resources are endless, and once the immediate ones are gone you can simply move on to new frontiers. Resources that were once plentiful and now are protected or regulated are furs, fertile native topsoil, clean air, virgin forests and lumber, clear water, iron ore, fish, wildlife and so on. The DNR is very strong and active in preserving and replenishing what Minnesota has naturally, and in keeping our landscape green.

Green and Blue Casserole

1 large onion, finely chopped
2 tablespoons butter
1 teaspoon salt
¼ teaspoon pepper
1 cup dairy sour cream
2 (16-ounce) cans cut green beans, drained
¼ cup crumbled blue cheese
½ cup buttered bread crumbs

Sauté onion in butter. Stir in seasonings and sour cream. Add beans; mix well. Put in casserole; sprinkle with blue cheese and bread crumbs. Bake, uncovered, at 350° for 20 to 25 minutes.

6 servings

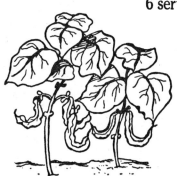

Keep Minnesota Green Beans

5 slices bacon, cut up
1 small onion, chopped
1 (10¾-ounce) can cream of mushroom soup
3 tablespoons cream
2 (16-ounce) cans green beans, drained
½ cup cubed cheese

Fry bacon and onion together until slightly browned; drain off drippings. Mix soup and cream together; add bacon and onion. Mix beans and cheese; add to soup mixture. Turn into casserole. Bake at 350° for about 30 minutes.

6 to 8 servings

Note: Four cups frozen or fresh beans, cooked, can be used for canned beans.

Thanks to the foresight of men like Charles Loring and Theodore Wirth, Minneapolis and St. Paul have one of the finest park systems in the world. There is more open space within the Twin Cities than there is in all of southwestern Minnesota. These lush, green oases are connected by parkways and paths, often crowded now with hikers, bikers, joggers, skaters and a profusion of people and pets of every sort, being propelled by every imaginable form of non-motorized conveyances. For a refreshing escape from the hustle, take the leisurely stern-wheeler, Jonathon Padelford, from Harriet Island to Ft. Snelling. You will barely realize you are in the midst of two cities as your eyes feast on the unspoiled green riverbanks en route. Later, the rest of you can feast on this succulent spinach dish.

Lush Green Spinach Bake

 2 (10-ounce) packages
   frozen chopped spinach
 6 eggs
 2 cups cottage cheese
 1 cup dairy sour cream
 1 cup margarine, cut into
   pieces
 8 ounces cubed Cheddar
   cheese

Thaw and drain spinach. Beat eggs; add cottage cheese, sour cream, margarine, cheese and spinach. Pour into 13x9x2-inch pan or baking dish. Bake, uncovered, at 350 for 1 hour.

6 to 8 servings

The Minnesota River starts at Big Stone Lake near Ortonville and wends its way 328 miles past Montevideo, Granite Falls and New Ulm. It takes a turn north at Mankato, going past St. Peter and Le Sueur, and finally stretches from there to Ft. Snelling State Park where it joins the Mississippi River. It was established as a recreational route and wildlife refuge in 1969, and the heritage of the lower valley is preserved in a living museum at Murphy's Landing near Shakopee. Like the Minnesota River banks, this spinach torte is rich and green.

Minnesota River Spinach Torte
"you can bank on it"

2 tablespoons olive oil
2 (10-ounce) packages
  frozen chopped spinach
1 medium onion, minced
2 cloves garlic, minced
¼ teaspoon nutmeg
1 (7-ounce) package lefse
2 (8-ounce) cans tomato
  sauce
1 cup grated Parmesan
  cheese
1 cup half & half

Coat bottom of 3-quart casserole (glass preferred to show the layers) with olive oil. Cook spinach as directed on package; drain. Sauté onion and garlic in remaining oil. Add spinach and nutmeg. Layer lefse, spinach mix, tomato sauce and cheese. Pour cream around edge of torte. Bake, covered, at 325° for 45 minutes.

6 servings

The Twin Cities nurtures a variety of cultural and educational opportunities for its youth. The Children's Museum in its new home in Bandana Square offers hands-on learning. The well-established Children's Theatre is internationally known, and national recognition was bestowed on CLIMB, Inc. in 1981, when it was proclaimed Best New Children's Theater Company in the country. Heart of the Beast Puppet Players is a favorite among all ages, and parks and schools offer many opportunities for youth involvement. A recommended way for the novice actor or actress to combat stage fright is to "just imagine the audience is a patch of cabbages."

Baked Cabbage
"a head start on drama"

1 large head white
  cabbage
1 (10¾-ounce) can cream
  of mushroom soup
1 cup milk or cream
  Salt and pepper to taste
1 cup shredded sharp
  Cheddar cheese

Chop cabbage. Combine soup and milk. Layer cabbage alternately with soup mixture in greased 2 to 3 quart baking dish; season. Bake at 350° for 30 minutes or until done. Sprinkle cheese on top; return to oven just until cheese melts.

4 to 6 servings

A stroll through the Renaissance Festival in Shakopee during an early fall weekend will transport you to the era of wandering minstrels and poets, kings and queens, knights in shining armor, acrobats and jugglers, Commedia del Arté troupes, belly dancers, stockades, jousting matches, horse races and a continuous panorama of other 17th century spectacles. Your taste buds can help round out the effect if you sample a few of the dozens of delicacies hawked by the food vendors. It's also an excellent chance to buy some of the fine handcrafts offered by costumed artists from many states.

Renaissance Red Cabbage

1 red cabbage, about 5 pounds
1 cup red wine
    Dash of vinegar
    Dash of salt
    Dash of black pepper
    Dash of ground cloves
2 teaspoons cinnamon
2 bay leaves
2 tablespoons sugar
5 tablespoons cranberry jelly
2 apples, peeled and cubed
½ cup apple sauce
    Salt and pepper

Shred cabbage on cucumber-slicer and combine with wine and vinegar in large kettle. Cover and bring to a boil. Reduce heat to low and cook about 20 minutes. Add spices, sugar, cranberry jelly and apples; cook about 40 minutes. Add applesauce and season with salt and pepper to taste.

5 to 6 servings

Note: Serve with venison roast.

Broccoli Bake

1 bunch fresh broccoli (or 2 (10-ounce) packages frozen broccoli, thawed), cut into bite-size pieces
1 (8-ounce) can sliced water chestnuts, drained
1 (10¾-ounce) can cream of celery soup
1 (2.8-ounce) can French fried onion rings

Place broccoli and water chestnuts in alternate layers in baking dish. Pour soup over top; sprinkle with onion rings. Bake at 350° for 30 to 45 minutes.

6 servings

Cauliflower Supreme

2 (10-ounce) packages frozen cauliflower or 1 head fresh cauliflower
1 (10¾-ounce) can cream of shrimp soup
½ cup dairy sour cream
¼ teaspoon salt
½ cup slivered almonds

Cook cauliflower; drain. Place in serving dish. Heat soup, sour cream and salt together; pour over cauliflower. Sprinkle with almonds. Serve immediately.

6 to 8 servings

Cauliflower Bake

1 large head cauliflower (4 cups) broken into bite-size pieces
1 (10¾-ounces) can cream of mushroom soup
½ cup shredded carrots
1 cup shredded Cheddar cheese
¼ cup milk
½ teaspoon dried basil
Pepper to taste

Cook cauliflower until tender; drain. Cool; place in 1½-quart casserole. Combine soup, carrots, cheese, milk, basil and pepper. Pour over cauliflower. Cover and refrigerate 3 to 24 hours. Bake, uncovered, at 350° for 40 minutes.

6 to 8 servings

A perennial figure on the St. Croix River scene was Alexander "Sandy" McDougal. A great Minnesota lumberman, he spent 60 winters felling trees, and came down the St. Croix on 49 consecutive spring log drives. He died in Mora in 1925.

Broccoli Casserole
"won't leave you stumped"

2 (10-ounce) packages frozen cut broccoli
2 eggs, beaten
1 (10¾-ounce) can Cheddar cheese soup
½ teaspoon dried oregano, crushed
1 (8-ounce) can stewed tomatoes, cut up
3 tablespoons grated Parmesan cheese

Cook broccoli in unsalted water 5 to 7 minutes until tender; drain well. Combine eggs, soup and oregano. Stir in tomatoes and broccoli. Turn mixture into 10x6x2-inch baking dish; sprinkle with cheese. Bake, uncovered, at 350° for about 30 minutes, until heated through.

8 servings

Pow-wows are spectacular events with Indians in full native costume pounding out the intricate rhythms of their traditional music and ceremonial dances. Minnesota Sioux and Chippewa gatherings draw participants from the entire country and Canada. A few prominent pow-wows are held at Mankato and Isle, the White Earth Indian Reservation near Detroit Lakes, the Bois Fort Reservation on Nett Lake near Orr and Cook, the Leech Lake and Red Lake Indian Reservations and at Kelliher. These festivities are often planned to coincide with the harvesting of blueberries and wild rice.

Wild Rice-Broccoli Bake
"pow-wow chow"

1 (6-ounce) package long
  grain wild rice mix
1 cup sliced celery
2 (10-ounce) packages
  frozen broccoli spears,
  cooked and drained
2 tablespoons butter
3 tablespoons flour
¼ teaspoon salt
2 cups milk
1 chicken bouillon cube
½ cup grated Parmesan
  cheese
1 tablespoon lemon juice

Cook rice according to package directions; stir in celery. Spread rice evenly in 5½-quart casserole. Arrange broccoli on top. Melt butter and stir in flour and salt; add milk and bouillon cube. Cook, stirring constantly until smooth and thickened. Stir in ¼ cup cheese and lemon juice. Pour over broccoli. Sprinkle remaining cheese on top. Bake at 375° for 20 minutes.

6 to 8 servings

Known as the "Rutabaga Capital of the World," the area around Askov once produced one-third of the rutabagas in the United States, and now commemorates this nice yellow vegetable with an annual festival. From the Swedish dialect, rutabaga literally means "root bag." This traditional Scandinavian Christmas dish will complement a holiday meal.

Rutabaga Casserole

2 medium rutabagas, peeled and diced (about 6 cups)
¼ cup fine dry bread crumbs
¼ cup cream
½ teaspoon nutmeg
1 teaspoon salt
2 eggs, beaten
3 tablespoons butter

Place rutabagas in saucepan with slightly salted water to barely cover; cook until soft. Drain and mash. Soak bread crumbs in cream and stir in nutmeg, salt and eggs. Combine with mashed rutabaga. Turn into a buttered 2½-quart casserole; dot top with butter. Bake at 350° for 1 hour or until lightly browned.

6 to 8 servings

Note: Turnips can be substituted for rutabagas.

"I'm as full of public spirit as a dog is full of fleas," proclaimed Oliver H. Kelly. This itch moved him to organize the Patrons of Husbandry, also called the Grange, in 1867. The organization was the first attempt of farmers to form a united front, and served as a social and cultural "farm fraternity." The Oliver H. Kelly farm near Elk River is called the "birthplace of organized agriculture in the United States."

Spicy Squash Bake
"agriculturally spirited"

4 to 5 cups butternut squash, peeled and cut into ¾-inch cubes
¼ cup finely chopped onion
1 clove garlic, minced
1 tablespoon butter
⅔ cup taco sauce
½ teaspoon salt
⅛ teaspoon pepper
½ cup shredded Cheddar cheese (about 4 ounces)

Steam squash 10 to 12 minutes. Meanwhile, cook onion and garlic in butter until tender. Stir in taco sauce, salt and pepper. Add squash cubes and stir. Place half of squash mixture in bottom of 1-quart casserole. Sprinkle with half of the cheese; top with remaining squash. Cover. Bake at 400° for 15 to 20 minutes. Uncover, top with remaining cheese and bake 5 minutes longer.

4 to 6 servings

The *New York Times* in 1956 referred to Minnesota as one of the most independent and politically unpredictable states. One of the best known of 3rd party politicians because of his fiery, humorous speeches was Ignatius Donnelley. Called the "Apostle of Protest," he was largely responsible for the formation of the Populist Party in 1891. This party lasted only five years, but the farmers' struggle for control and protection continued in the Farmer-Labor party, electing Floyd B. Nelson governor in 1932 and 1934. Due in part to the efforts of Hubert H. Humphrey, this party merged with the Democratic Party in 1944, emerging as the DFL. This is a prime example of Minnesota's independent political nature.

Eggplant-Potato Bake
"a mighty merger"

2 pounds potatoes, peeled
2 onions, sliced
2 large eggplants, peeled and sliced
1 tablespoon vegetable oil
8 ounces Cheddar cheese, shredded
Salt and pepper

Partially cook potatoes in boiling salted water 10 minutes; drain and slice. Fry onions in oil just until soft. In casserole, layer the 3 vegetables, topping each layer with cheese, salt and pepper (top layer should be eggplant with cheese topping). Bake, covered, at 375° for 1½ hours or until golden brown.

8 servings

147

The Festival of Nations is Minnesota's largest ethnic celebration. Fifty-five ethnic groups gather annually in the St. Paul Civic Center to combine their influences in a phantasmagoria of music, dance, folk art, food and cultural activities for the edification and enjoyment of thousands who attend this round-the-world journey under one roof. First held in 1932 and called "Folk Festival," the event is an outgrowth of the year-round work of the International Institute.

Zucchini Mexicali
"a festival of flavors"

¼ cup vegetable oil
4 cups thinly sliced zucchini
1 cup coarsely shredded carrot
1 cup chopped onion
¾ cup chopped celery
½ medium green pepper, cut into thin strips
½ teaspoon garlic salt
¼ teaspoon dried basil
Dash of pepper
⅓ cup taco sauce
2 teaspoons prepared mustard
2 medium tomatoes, cut into wedges

Heat oil in 10-inch skillet or wok. Combine all vegetables with salt, basil and pepper; cook, covered, over high heat 4 minutes or until vegetables are tender-crisp. Stir occasionally. Combine taco sauce and mustard; stir into vegetables. Add tomato wedges. Cook, uncovered, 3 to 5 minutes.

4 to 6 servings

"Tunnels in the sky," the maze-like network of skyways connecting major buildings in the downtown areas of the Twin Cities, provide us with another claim to fame. St. Paul has three miles of skyways but is now topped by Minneapolis, which currently has more than any other city in the world. What gives rise to Minnesota's high-struttin' ways? Why, our high-interest clime, of course. We are a people who love to look at and discuss the prevailing conditions at great length, but not necessarily to suffer the slings and arrows of outrageous weather. This same sensible rationality underlies other overhead configurations as well, such as the first all-enclosed shopping center, Southdale in Edina, Town Square in St. Paul, the world's largest enclosed park, and the Mall of America, the world's largest enclosed mall.

Skyway Tostadas
"shortcut to a tasty meal"

1 medium zucchini, thinly sliced
1 medium onion, thinly sliced
1 (3-ounce) can sliced mushrooms, drained
¼ cup chopped celery
2 tablespoons chopped green pepper
8 corn tostadas (crisp tortillas)
1 tomato, chopped
1 cup Cheddar cheese, shredded
½ cup dairy sour cream

Simmer vegetables 8 to 10 minutes. Drain. Heat oven to 350°. On cookie sheet or in cake pan, place tostadas. Evenly distribute vegetables over tostadas. Top with tomatoes and cheese. Place in oven 3 to 5 minutes, just until cheese is melted. Top with sour cream and serve.

Makes 8 tostadas

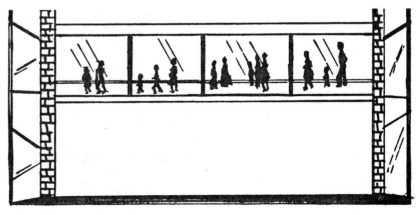

149

A banquet of color and fragrance blankets the 650 acres of the Minnesota Landscape Arboretum in Chaska. Run by the University of Minnesota Horticulture Department, it develops many plants especially for Minnesota. Hardy blueberries and the Northern Lights Azalea are two that have been bred to survive our climate. Perham, as the testing ground for these flowering shrubs, is destined to be the azalea capital of the Midwest. In time these horticultural experiments will be as tried and true as Max's Brown Beans.

Max's Brown Beans
"tried and true"

1 pound ground beef
½ cup chopped onion
½ pound bacon, crisply fried and crumbled
1 (28-ounce) can Bush's baked beans
½ cup molasses
¼ cup packed brown sugar
1½ teaspoons prepared mustard

Brown ground beef and onion together; drain. Place beans in casserole. Add ground beef and remaining ingredients. Cover and bake at 325° for 35 to 40 minutes.

6 to 8 servings

Note: Excellent do-ahead. Can be frozen or chilled and heated in microwave. Easily doubled.

Though Minnesota is seldom considered the "Wild West," Zimmerman doesn't care. It celebrates the wild west with zest. So does Park Rapids, which mounts an annual professional World Championship Rodeo every July 4th. Rip-roaring rodeos are also kicked off by Buffalo, Granite Falls and St. Paul.

Ride-'Em Baked Beans
"lasso even the most bull-headed"

1 large onion, diced
1 pound bacon, diced
1 (28-ounce) can Bush's baked beans
2 (15-ounce) cans kidney beans, drained
1 (15-ounce) can butter beans, drained
1 cup catsup
1 cup packed brown sugar
2 tablespoons vinegar
2 teaspoons liquid smoke
Salt and pepper to taste

Fry onion and bacon together; drain off drippings. Combine with remaining ingredients. Heat through or cook in crockpot on low for 4 to 9 hours.

6 to 8 servings

Note: Can add 1 pound ground beef, browned and drained.

Jane Gray Swisshelm was a fiery and determined abolitionist and feminist in the 1850's. She ran the St. Cloud newspaper called *The Visitor,* and had no reservations about candid, unequivocal campaigning for her causes, both in print and in lecture. When an outraged prominent citizen threatened a libel suit against her, she agreed to quit attacking him in *The Visitor.* The following week she changed the name of her paper to *The St. Cloud Democrat* and zealously resumed her crusade. She was not deterred when an angry mob broke into her office, threw her printing press into the river and burned her in effigy. She left Minnesota when her principles led her into the Civil War as a nurse.

Spunky Twice-Baked Potatoes
"a dish with conviction"

7 large baking potatoes
½ to ¾ cup milk
1 (3-ounce) package
   cream cheese, softened
6 tablespoons butter
⅛ teaspoon garlic powder
⅛ to ¼ teaspoon white
   pepper
   Salt
6 ounces Cheddar cheese,
   shredded

Scrub, dry, pierce and bake potatoes at 425° for 1 hour. About 10 minutes before potatoes are done, blend milk, cream cheese, butter, garlic powder and pepper until smooth. Add more milk or butter if necessary to get the right consistency. Heat in a saucepan; do not boil. When potatoes are done, remove and immediately slice lengthwise, leaving shell intact. Spoon out cooked potato into large bowl; salt to taste. With electric mixer, beat potatoes slightly and gradually add cream cheese mixture. Spoon mixture into shells of 6 potatoes; top with cheese. Heat in oven for about 20 minutes or microwave on high power until cheese is melted.

6 servings

Waterways have dramatically affected the history of our state. When the French found Minnesota's rivers, they found mobility, beaver and muskrat pelts and wealth. The British took control in 1763 and maintained it until 1812. As Americans began arriving, Ft. Snelling was built and used as a stopping place for river traffic. The Minnesota Territorial Convention met in Stillwater on March 3, 1849, at which time 61 delegates chose the name of Minnesota. Congress then declared it a territory, and Stillwater became known as the birthplace of Minnesota. Soon land was purchased from the Indians and settlement began. On May 11, 1858, Minnesota became the nation's 32nd state.

Stately Parmesan Potatoes
"seal of approval"

6 unpeeled potatoes, quartered
¼ cup flour
¼ cup grated Parmesan cheese
¾ teaspoon salt
⅛ teaspoon pepper
⅓ cup butter

Mix flour, cheese, salt and pepper in a paper or plastic bag. Add potatoes and shake until covered thoroughly. Melt butter in 13x9x2-inch pan. Add potatoes. Bake at 375° for 1 hour, turning potatoes once or twice.

4 to 6 servings

The "Lady in the Lake" and the "Brown's Valley Man" would certainly make a unique couple. Our skeletal lady was unearthed in 1931 and is believed to have drowned in a glacial lake some 20,000 years ago. Our man is a mere youngster of about 12,000 years, discovered in 1933; but some women do prefer younger men. Incidentally, the "Lady in the Lake" is archaeologically known as the "Minnesota Man." She may not be very well-endowed, but isn't this a rather low archaeological dig?

Earthy Potatoes
"you'll dig 'em"

8 to 12 potatoes, boiled, peeled and shredded (or 2 (32-ounce) packages frozen shredded potatoes)
1½ cups shredded Cheddar cheese
1 large onion, chopped and sauteed
 Salt and pepper
1 pint whipping cream

Layer half of ingredients in 2-quart casserole. Repeat layers; top with cream. Bake, uncovered, at 350° for 1 to 1½ hours.

8 to 10 servings

"Cows, colleges and contentment." This was the motto of Northfield for many years. In the midst of a rich dairy area, it was called "Holstein Capital of America." Two nationally respected private colleges, Carleton and St. Olaf, endow Northfield with much of its reputation as a progressive and creative town. Ole E. Rolvaag, author of the classic *Giants in the Earth*, was a professor at St. Olaf. The town also contains more than 70 buildings listed on the National Register of Historic Places.

Creamed Potatoes
"high on the table of contentment"

6 cups cooked, cubed potatoes
¼ cup chopped onion
1 (10¾-ounce) can cream of chicken soup
1 (5-ounce) can evaporated milk
1 cup cubed Velveeta cheese

Combine all ingredients in pan or casserole and let stand 8 hours or overnight in refrigerator. Bake at 350° for 1 hour.

6 servings

Summertime may mean "Easy Livin'" to most of the state, but it is a time when Brainerd celebrates "Life in the Fast Lane." International Raceway, formerly known as Donneybrook, draws famous cars, cycles and drivers from far and wide. Many celebrities, including Paul Newman, have peeled their way around the illustrious racetrack in pursuit of the "Big Potato."

Speedy Spuds
"bound to make you a Big Wheel"

2 pounds frozen hash brown potatoes, thawed
½ cup butter, melted
1 teaspoon salt
¼ teaspoon pepper
½ cup chopped onion
1 (10¾-ounce) can cream of chicken soup
1 (8-ounce) carton dairy sour cream
2 cups shredded Cheddar cheese
Topping;
1½ cups crushed corn flakes
¼ cup butter, melted

Combine all ingredients except topping. Spread in 13x9x2-inch pan. Combine corn flakes and butter; sprinkle on potato mixture. Bake at 300° for 1¼ hours.

8 to 10 servings

Hint: Make up in advance and freeze. Thaw completely before baking.

156

Sigurd F. Olson lived and breathed the essence of his writings as an outdoorsman and guide around the Ely and Lake of the Woods area, known as "canoe country." His profound empathy with the wilderness along with his academic abilities as a professor and dean made him a much-loved and highly-respected naturalist and ecologist. Some of his best known works are *The Singing Wilderness, The Hidden Forest, Reflections from the North Country* and *Runes of the North.*

Wild Rice Casserole
"a taste of the wild"

1 cup uncooked wild rice
1 onion, chopped
3 stalks celery, chopped
1 teaspoon seasoned salt
½ cup white wine
2 tablespoons butter
1 quart chicken broth
  Salt and pepper

Combine all ingredients and place in casserole. Bake, covered, at 325° for 2 hours.

4 to 6 servings

Hint: Make double and freeze one. Freezes well and heats up nicely in microwave.

Minnesota Public Radio (MPR) is a statewide public radio station broadcasting from 19 strategic spots. It holds the remarkable distinction of rallying the largest public radio membership support anywhere—another indication of Minnesota's dedication to artistic propagation. MPR produces many innovative programs for national transmission, including Garrison Keillor's "American Radio Company," replacing the immensely popular "Prairie Home Companion." You'll muster plenty of public support of your own when your kitchen's airwaves waft a whiff of this stuff.

Prairie Home Stuffing
"the right companion for your bird"

3 quarts bread cubes
½ cup margarine, melted
¼ cup bacon drippings, melted
1 onion, finely chopped
1 cup celery tops, chopped
¼ cup parsley, chopped
Salt and pepper
1 teaspoon poultry seasoning
3 eggs, beaten
1 teaspoon sage (or to taste)
Chicken broth

Combine all ingredients using just enough broth to moisten; toss together until mixed.

Makes enough to stuff a 12-pound fowl

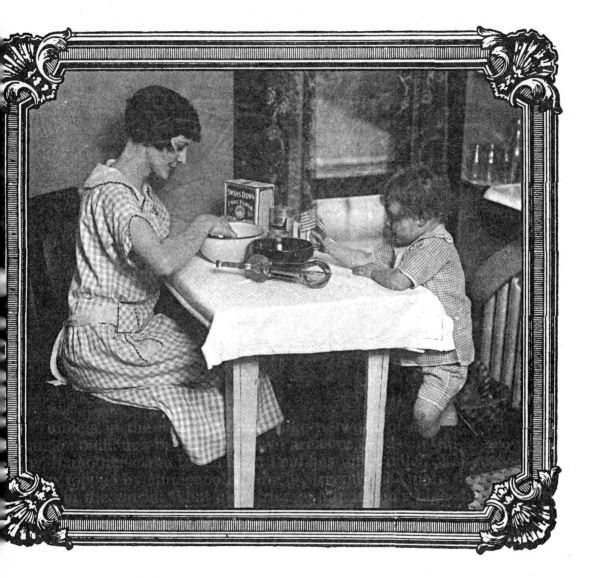

Metro Land Desserts

The diary of a St. Anthony housewife in the 1850's disclosed that she made 21 pies every week, or one per meal. The importance of sweets in early menus is evident in cookbooks which were dominated by recipes for desserts. In that tradition, we offer the following:

Traditional Peach Pie

2 cups sugar
½ cup flour
¼ teaspoon nutmeg
½ cup butter
6 to 8 large peaches, peeled
½ cup water

Heat oven to 450°. Combine sugar, flour, nutmeg and butter. Divide into fourths. Sprinkle ¼ on bottom of each of two 9-inch pie pans. Cut peaches in half; place over crust, cut side down. Sprinkle remaining crumbs on top, ¼ on each pie. Sprinkle top of each pie with ¼ cup water. Bake 10 minutes; reduce oven temperature to 350° and bake 30 minutes longer.

Makes 2 (9-inch) pies

Short-Crust Pastry

3 cups all-purpose flour
1¼ cups shortening
1 teaspoon salt
1 egg
5½ tablespoons water
1 teaspoon vinegar

Mix flour, shortening and salt together until very fine. Beat egg, water and vinegar together. Make a little well in flour and add liquid. Mix until well blended and dough forms a ball. Roll out on floured pastry cloth.

Makes 2 double crusts

The name of James J. Hill criss-crosses Minnesota history just as his railroad tracks criss-cross our landscape. As his Great Northern Railway burgeoned across the state in the 1870's, "Jim Hill Towns" popped up every 6 or 7 miles along the lines to provide water for the steam engines, thus conferring on him the title of "Empire Builder." This tycoon had his finger in many pies, but none more irresistible than this mellow chocolate one.

Hershey Bar Pie
"a hill of heaven"

1 (9-inch) graham cracker crust
6 (1.45-ounce) almond Hershey chocolate bars
18 marshmallows
½ cup milk
2 cups whipping cream, whipped

Prepare pie crust. Melt chocolate and marshmallows with milk in double boiler over hot water; cool. Fold in whipped cream. Spoon into crust. Refrigerate at least 8 hours. Garnish with additional whipped cream and shaved chocolate, if desired.

Makes 1 (9-inch) pie

A Minnesota woman, Dr. Jeanette Piccard, is recognized as the first woman in space. In 1934 she rode a high-altitude helium-filled balloon 11 miles into the stratosphere. With the following recipe, the humble rhubarb stalk reaches heavenly heights.

Mile-High Rhubarb Pie
"gives rise to lofty praise"

Crust:
- 1 cup all-purpose flour
- 2 tablespoons powdered sugar
- ½ cup butter
- Pinch of salt

Filling:
- 2½ cups cut-up rhubarb
- 1⅓ cups sugar
- 3 egg yolks
- 2 tablespoons flour
- ⅓ cup milk

Meringue:
- 3 egg whites
- ¼ teaspoon cream of tartar
- 6 tablespoons sugar
- ½ teaspoon vanilla

Heat oven to 350°. Mix crust ingredients together and press into 8-inch pie pan. Bake 20 minutes. Combine filling ingredients in saucepan, cook until thick; pour into baked crust. Heat oven to 400°. Beat egg whites and cream of tartar until foamy; gradually add sugar and beat until stiff but not dry. Fold in vanilla. Spread over filling; seal edges of meringue to crust. Bake about 10 minutes, until meringue is browned.

Makes 1 (8-inch) pie

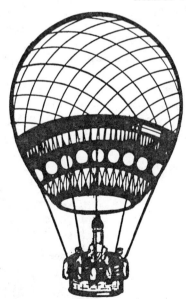

The countryside is all abuzz with the veritable beehive of activity arising from the many apiaries which dot Minnesota's rural areas. Those fuzzy little busybodies industriously convert the nectar from almost anything that blooms into an amazing array of honeys, each with its own distinct flavor — clover, alfalfa, watermelon and buckwheat, to name a few. To bee or not to bee in Minnesota when it freezes is the question, and many beekeepers make a beeline south for the winter. If you're not one of them, one taste of this scrumptious pie will tell you, snow or no snow, that you're in the land of milk (and related dairy products) and honey.

Greek Cheese and Honey Pie

Sesame seed crust:
- **1** tablespoon sesame seeds
- **1** cup all-purpose flour
- **⅓** cup butter or margarine, softened
- **1** tablespoon sugar
- **¼** teaspoon salt

Filling:
- **2** (8-ounce) packages cream cheese, softened
- **2** eggs
- **½** cup sugar
- **½** cup honey
- **½** cup whipping cream
- **1** teaspoon grated lemon peel
- **¼** teaspoon ground nutmeg

Heat sesame seeds in ungreased skillet over medium heat, stirring occasionally until golden. Heat oven to 475°. In mixing bowl, mix remaining crust ingredients with toasted seed until blended. Press firmly and evenly against bottom and side of 9-inch pie plate. Bake 5 minutes. Beat cream cheese in large mixer bowl on medium speed until creamy. Add remaining ingredients; beat until light and fluffy. Pour into crust. Bake 40 to 50 minutes, until firm. Cool; refrigerate until served.

Makes 1 (9-inch) pie

Note: Both crust and pie can be made very easily in a food processor.

"Big Cheese" gained new meaning with Pine Island's 1914 entry in the State Fair. Their cheese, shipped by flatcar, weighed 6,000 pounds and was the largest ever produced from one day's whey. This cheesecake is so delicious it will surely blow you away!

State Fair Cheesecake
"a huge success"

Crust:
1 cup vanilla wafer crumbs
3 tablespoons butter, melted
Filling:
3 (8-ounce) packages cream cheese, softened
1 cup sugar
5 eggs
2 teaspoons vanilla
Topping:
3 cups dairy sour cream
6 tablespoons sugar
1 to 2 tablespoons Amaretto

Heat oven to 350°. Combine crumbs and butter; press on bottom of 9-inch springform pan. Bake 8 to 10 minutes. Cool. Reduce oven temperature to 300°. Combine filling ingredients; mix well. Pour into crust. Bake 1½ hours. Let cheesecake stand 10 minutes. Combine topping ingredients; pour over cheesecake. Bake 10 minutes longer.

10 to 12 servings

The Minneapolis-St. Paul rivalry ran rampant in the 1880's with an all-out war to record the largest population. Census takers were kidnapped, both cities accused the other of padding the census, and the newspapers fed the furor. When finally a new census was ordered, flagrant transgressions were found on both sides. St. Paul enumerated 325 houses not on the map, 14 families living in the Bank of Minnesota Building, 25 persons in the barber shop of a St. Paul hotel, 245 in the Union Depot, 120 in one small house and 35 in a dime museum. Minneapolis included in their totals long lists of people buried in cemeteries and hundreds of other improper attempts to swell the rolls. St. Paul newspapers referred to Minneapolis as "Padville" or "Pad City." The public of both cities readily forgave these transgressions, however, considering them nothing more than over-zealous "Booster Spirit."

Padville Cheesecake

1 (9-inch) graham cracker crust
½ cup packed brown sugar
2 tablespoons flour
¼ teaspoon salt
2 (8-ounce) packages cream cheese, softened
1 teaspoon vanilla
4 eggs, separated
1 cup cream or rich milk
Nutmeg, optional

Heat oven to 325°. Combine brown sugar, flour and salt; thoroughly blend with cream cheese. Add vanilla and egg yolks; beat throroughly. Stir in cream. Beat egg whites until stiff; fold into cheese mixture. Pour filling into crust; sprinkle with nutmeg. Bake for about 1 hour, until center is firm.

6 to 8 servings

The "seven minutes that shook Northfield" occurred on September 7, 1876, with the attempted holdup of the First National Bank by the notorious James-Younger gang. The townspeople sprang into action and prevented the robbery, but several were killed. A posse of nearly 1000 men captured the Youngers in the marshes near Madelia, making them the most famous inmates in the new Stillwater prison. The James brothers escaped to the hills of Blue Mounds, eventually making their way back to Missouri. Imagine the embarrassment of the Chaska sheriff when he realized that these were the strangers who had joined him in a poker game a few days earlier. The largest Minnesota festival outside the Twin Cities, the "Defeat of Jesse James Days" draws over 95,000 people yearly to ogle the bullet holes in the bank, to applaud a lively re-enactment of the historic event and to otherwise commemorate the heroism of Northfield's ancestors.

Hero Poppyseed Cake

1 (18¼-ounce) package
 lemon cake mix
 (without pudding)
1 (4-serving size) package
 lemon instant pudding
 mix
½ cup vegetable oil
1 cup cold water
4 eggs
¼ cup poppy seeds

Heat oven to 350°. Combine cake mix, pudding mix, oil and water; blend well. Add eggs, 1 at a time, mixing well after each. Add poppy seeds. Pour into greased and floured loaf pan. Bake 40 to 50 minutes. Cool in pan 10 minutes; remove to wire rack to cool completely.

Makes 1 loaf cake

Fort Snelling is unusual in that it was never engaged in an actual battle, so it was free to entertain other functions. The later famous slave, Dred Scott, was married in the Round Tower in 1837. Later, in 1864, a mysterious luminous canvas bag could be seen hovering 300 feet over the Tower for 30 time-suspending minutes as Count Zeppelin conducted test runs of his Zeppelin balloons. Still a bustling center of all sorts of activities, from polo matches to old-style blacksmithing and dramatic performances, it is also open for tours of its beautifully restored buildings.

Round Tower Red Cake

½ cup butter, softened
1½ cups sugar
2 eggs
2 ounces red food coloring
2 teaspoons unsweetened cocoa powder
2¼ cups cake flour
½ teaspoon salt
1 cup buttermilk
1 teaspoon vanilla
1 teaspoon soda in 1 teaspoon vinegar
Frosting:
3 tablespoons flour
1 cup milk
1 cup powdered sugar
1 cup butter or margarine, softened
1 tablespoon vanilla

Grease and flour 2 layer cake pans. Heat oven to 350°. Cream butter, sugar and eggs. Add remaining ingredients in order; mix thoroughly. Pour into prepared pans. Bake about 30 minutes. Cool layers on wire racks. For frosting, cook flour and milk together in double boiler over hot water until thick. Let cool completely. Cream sugar, butter and vanilla until fluffy. Barely blend into cooled mixture until it is the thickness of oatmeal. Spread on cake.

Makes 1 (2-layer) cake

The Laurentian Divide is responsible for Minnesota being called "The Mother of Three Seas." A high granite ridge running from a point near Grand Rapids up the North Shore, it causes our rivers to flow in three directions away from it. The Red River runs north to Hudson Bay; the Minnesota, Mississippi and St. Croix Rivers run to the Gulf of Mexico; and the St. Louis River and North Shore streams run to Lake Superior. In fact, all waters flow out of Minnesota, and none flow in.

Three Seas Cake
"make it in the pan"

3 cups all-purpose flour
2 cups sugar
⅓ cup unsweetened cocoa
   powder
1 teaspoon salt
2 teaspoon baking soda
¾ cup vegetable oil
2 teaspoons vanilla
2 tablespoons vinegar
2 cups water

Heat oven to 350°. Combine dry ingredients in ungreased 13x9x2-inch pan. Make 3 wells in mixture. Put oil in one well, vanilla in one well and vinegar in one well. Pour water over all and mix until smooth. Bake 25 to 30 minutes. Frost with Chocolate Chip Frosting.

Makes 1 (13x9-inch) cake

Chocolate Chip Frosting

¾ cup sugar
2½ tablespoons butter
3 tablespoons milk
½ cup chocolate chips

Combine sugar, butter and milk in saucepan. Bring to a full boil, stirring constantly. Stir in chocolate chips. Remove from heat. Beat until thick enough to spread.

Makes frosting for 1 (13x9-inch) cake

Itchy, twitchy, creepy, crawly. It's spring and you've been enjoying a lovely and leisurely nature hike when you discover that a small denizen of that woodland paradise has chosen you to go home with. He's the friendly woodtick, a devoted pal who'll stick with you through thin and thicket. If you opt to reject his offer of a truly close relationship, you'll find he's not that easy to forget. The tickle of the tick remains long after he's gone, and you're sure he's left friends behind, a feeling which invariably instigates the nervous tic hunt. But soon the call of the great outdoors will have you out there once again, smelling the flowers, feeling the breezes and listening to the tick talk.

Tick-Tock Cake
"chocolate chip delight"

1½ cups boiling water
1 cup rolled oats
1 cup packed brown sugar
1 cup granulated sugar
½ cup margarine, softened
2 large eggs
1¾ cups all-purpose flour
1 teaspoon soda
½ teaspoon salt
1 tablespoon unsweetened cocoa powder
1 (6-ounce) package chocolate chips
¾ cup chopped nuts, optional
Powdered sugar

Pour water over oats and let stand 10 minutes. Heat oven to 350°. Add sugars, margarine and eggs to oats; mix well. Add dry ingredients and mix well. Stir in chocolate chips and nuts. Pour into greased 13x9x2-inch pan. Bake about 40 minutes. When cool, sprinkle with powdered sugar; needs no frosting.

Makes 1 (13x9-inch) cake

It's amazing that a river 2500 miles long and up to a mile wide can have the modest beginnings of the Mississippi River. The headwaters of "Old Man River" are found in Itasca State Park among 32,000 acres of stately trees, including Minnesota's only stand of virgin forest and the largest Norway Pine, which is about 120 feet around and over 300 years old. Tourists young and old are tickled by the trickle of "the Mighty Mississippi" as they perform the ritual of stepping across the headwaters to the click of cameras, then continue on their way into the primeval forests to hunt blueberries.

Itasca Blueberry Cake

1 cup sugar
½ cup shortening
2 eggs
½ cup dairy sour cream
1½ teaspoons vanilla
2 cups all-purpose flour
2 teaspoons baking powder
½ teaspoon ginger
¼ teaspoon baking soda
½ teaspoon salt
1 pint fresh blueberries
⅓ cup sugar

Grease and flour 13x9x2-inch pan. Heat oven to 350°. In large mixer bowl, cream 1 cup sugar and shortening together; add eggs, sour cream and vanilla. Combine flour, baking powder, ginger, soda and salt; add to egg mixture. Mix well at medium speed. (If too thick up to ¼ cup milk can be added.) Carefully fold in blueberries. Pour into prepared pan. Sprinkle ⅓ cup sugar on top. Bake about 40 minutes. Best served with whipped cream.

Makes 1 (13x9-inch) cake

Apple Blossom Scenic Drive is one of two official state scenic drives. It takes you from Pickwick, named after Charles Dickens, to La Crescent, the Apple Capital of Minnesota. You can pick varieties of apples such as the hardy Wealthy or the tart crisp Haralson at any of the apple farms along this route. Here is a recipe to make any Minnesota apple even more appealing.

Twice Baked German Apple Cake
"heavy and sweet"

Cake:
1 cup sugar
1 cup all-purpose flour
¼ cup butter
1 teaspoon baking powder
1 teaspoon vanilla
1 large egg
4 large apples
Topping:
3 tablespoons sugar
3 tablespoons butter, melted
1 teaspoon cinnamon
1 large egg

Heat oven to 350°. Cut sugar and flour into butter. Add baking powder, vanilla and egg. Mix until it resembles cornmeal. Press mixture into a well-buttered springform pan. Peel, core and slice apples. Arrange in layers on top of crumb mixture. Bake for about 45 minutes. Meanwhile, make the topping: combine sugar, butter and cinnamon. When butter is cool enough, beat in egg. When cake comes out of oven, pour topping over cake. Bake 25 to 30 minutes longer or until top is firm.

Makes 1 (9-inch) cake

If knowledge is power, we can pride ourselves in a mighty state! Only about medium-sized in population, Minnesota allocates one of the highest expenditures for education and can boast one of the lowest illiteracy rates. The University of Minnesota has 5 campuses and one of the largest enrollments in the nation. We also have 7 state universities, 13 community colleges, 24 private colleges and 33 area vo-tech schools. All these fine seats of learning assure our future status as a great "State of Mind."

Fruit-of-All-Knowledge Cake
"a real apple polisher"

1 cup shortening
1 cup granulated sugar
½ cup packed brown sugar
2 eggs
1 cup buttermilk
2½ cups all-purpose flour
1 teaspoon baking soda
1 teaspoon baking powder
1 teaspoon cinnamon
1 teaspoon salt
1 teaspoon vanilla
2 cups diced apple
Topping:
¼ cup granulated sugar
¼ cup packed brown sugar
½ teaspoon cinnamon
½ cup shredded coconut
½ cup chocolate or butterscotch chips

Grease and flour 13x9x2-inch pan. Heat oven to 350°. Cream shortening and sugars. Add eggs and buttermilk; blend. Stir dry ingredients together; sprinkle a little of the mixture over the apples and toss. Blend remaining dry ingredients into creamed mixture. Stir in vanilla and apple; mix well. Pour into prepared pan. Combine topping ingredients; sprinkle over batter. Bake 45 to 50 minutes.

Makes 1 (13x9-inch) cake

Minnesotan Bob Dylan has left an indelible mark on the music scene. Raised in Hibbing on the Iron Range, his early performances took place unceremoniously in small bars and coffeehouses in Dinkytown and on the West Bank in Minneapolis. His unique arrangements of guitar, harmonica and voice produced a very distinctive and much-imitated sound. And none can dispute the impact that his multi-topical lyrics had upon the world. Indeed he was the social conscience of the 60's.

Hummingbird Cake
"lyrical"

3 cups all-purpose flour
2 cups sugar
1 teaspoon baking soda
1 teaspoon salt
1 teaspoon cinnamon
3 eggs, beaten
1 cup vegetable oil
1 teaspoon vanilla
1 (8-ounce) can crushed
   pineapple
2 cups chopped banana
1 cup chopped pecans
Frosting:
1 (8-ounce) package
   cream cheese
½ cup butter, softened
1 pound powdered sugar
   (about 4 cups)
1 teaspoon vanilla

Grease and flour three 9-inch round cake pans. Heat oven to 350°. Combine dry ingredients; add eggs and oil, stirring until moistened - do not beat! Stir in vanilla, pineapple, bananas and pecans. Spoon into prepared pans. Bake 25 to 30 minutes, until toothpick inserted in center comes out clean. Cool 10 minutes in pan; remove and cool completely on wire rack. For frosting, cream butter and cream cheese together; blend in powdered sugar and vanilla. Beat until smooth and fluffy. Frost cooled cake.

Makes 1 (9-inch 3-layer) cake

The first locomotive to run in Minnesota was the "William Crooks," making its maiden voyage on July 2, 1862, between St. Paul and St. Anthony. The first railroad line out of Minneapolis had just 3 stops, one being the maidenly Minnehaha Depot, known as "The Princess." Operated from the 1870's to 1963, this 16-mile line once carried commuters downtown and picnickers and visitors to Minnehaha Park and Falls for only 5¢. The ornate Victorian station, now operated by the Minnesota Historical Society, has plenty of gingerbread trim and is just dandy!

Gingerbread Dandy

1½ cups all-purpose flour
½ cup sugar
1 teaspoon baking soda
½ teaspoon ground cloves
½ teaspoon ground ginger
½ teaspoon cinnamon
   Pinch of salt
1 egg
½ cup butter, softened
½ cup boiling water
   Creamy Date Topping:
½ cup finely chopped dates
2 tablespoons sugar
2 tablespoons orange juice
½ cup whipping cream

Heat oven to 350°. Combine dry ingredients; blend in egg and butter. Add boiling water and mix until blended. Pour into greased 9x9x2-inch pan. Bake 25 to 30 minutes. Cool. For topping, combine dates, sugar and orange juice. Whip cream until soft peaks form; fold in date mixture. Serve a dollop of topping of each piece of gingerbread.

9 servings

The first Minnesota license plates were issued in 1907 to a whopping total of 500 cars. In 1984, there were 2.3 million cars bearing the inscription "MINNESOTA ... LAND OF 10,000 LAKES." This slogan was slated to be removed from the plates in 1975, because state officials had decided it cluttered the plates and obscured the numbers. But the citizens arose with such a furor of protest that the decision was reversed and the familiar phrase remained.

Fresh Fruit Dessert Plate
"your license to fruition"

1 (14-ounce) can sweetened condensed milk
½ cup dairy sour cream
¼ cup reconstituted lemon juice
1 teaspoon vanilla
½ cup margarine or butter, softened
¼ cup packed light brown sugar
1 cup flour
¼ cup quick-cooking oats
¼ cup finely chopped walnuts
Assorted fresh or canned fruits: strawberries, grapes, kiwi fruit, oranges, pineapple, banana, etc.
Mint leaves, optional

Heat oven to 375°. In medium bowl, combine condensed milk, sour cream, lemon juice and vanilla; mix well and chill. In large bowl, beat margarine and brown sugar until fluffy. Add flour, oats and nuts; blend well. Using lightly oiled pizza pan or cookie sheet, press dough into a 12-inch circle, forming a rim around the edge. Prick with fork and bake 10 to 12 minutes or until golden brown; cool. Spoon cooled filling evenly onto crust. Arrange well-drained fruit on top of filling, starting at center and working out in circles, alternating fruits. Chill.

8 to 10 servings

"Blueberry Country" abides in the green pine forest around Itasca State Park. Ladyslippers and trillium bloom in the spring, giving way to the profusion of wild blueberries that peak in late July. Then the people of Lake George rejoice over those succulent little woodland gems with a Blueberry Festival during which a Blueberry King and Queen preside over a Blueberry Ball. The festivities may be wild, but the main attraction is still the wild blueberries . . . yours for the picking.

Blueberry Betty

4 cups fresh blueberries
2 cups fresh bread
  crumbs
3 tablespoons butter or
  margarine, melted
½ cup packed brown
  sugar
1 teaspoon cinnamon
1 tablespoon grated
  lemon peel
2 tablespoons lemon juice
¼ cup hot water
  Whipped cream

Rinse blueberries and drain well. Toss crumbs with melted butter. Combine sugar, cinnamon and lemon peel. Sprinkle ⅓ of bread crumb mixture in bottom of a well-buttered 1½-quart baking dish. Cover with half of the blueberries and sprinkle with half of the sugar mixture. Repeat the layers: crumbs, blueberries and sugar. Top with remaining ⅓ of crumbs. Combine lemon juice and hot water; pour evenly over the top. Bake at 350° for 30 minutes. Serve warm with whipped cream.

6 servings

The Jeffers Petroglyphs, north of Windom, are a collection of more than 2000 rock carvings made by several different Indian groups over a period of some 5000 years. One of the largest petroglyph areas in the world, it is carved into a 20-mile-long outcrop of red quartzite in the midst of a virgin plain. The figures of animal, human and abstract designs vary in size from a few inches to several feet, and depict a rich and vanished past. Incidentally, the white man has occupied Minnesota for only 5% of its human history.

Rhubarb Dessert
"lose your stick figure"

6 cups cut-up rhubarb
2 cups sugar
2 tablespoons flour
½ teaspoon baking soda
½ teaspoon baking powder
⅔ cup shortening, melted
1½ cups rolled oats
1½ cups packed brown sugar
1½ cups all-purpose flour

Heat oven to 350°. Mix rhubarb, sugar and flour. Put in greased 13x9x2-inch pan. Combine remaining ingredients; sprinkle on top of rhubarb mixture. Bake 30 to 40 minutes.

15 servings

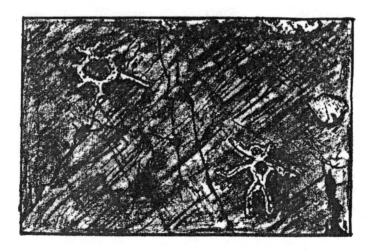

International Falls is often thought to be the coldest spot in Minnesota, but that notoriety actually belongs to Roseau. Other laurels go to International Falls, however. For instance, it does have the largest paper mills in the country. Its forests yield bounties of raspberries, blueberries and juneberries, and a springtime maple sugar harvest. Minnesota's largest prehistoric Indian burial mound is also nearby, with a circumference of 325 feet and a height of 45 feet. This dessert is perfect for the International Falls area, but not because it's borderline!

Top of the State Juneberry Dessert

1 quart (or less) juneberries
½ cup granulated sugar
1 tablespoon cornstrach
½ cup water
Topping:
1 cup packed brown sugar
1 cup flour
½ teaspoon salt
⅓ cup margarine

Combine berries, granulated sugar, cornstarch and water in 9x9x2-inch pan. Combine topping ingredients and sprinkle over berries. Bake at 350° for 45 minutes.

9 servings

Scandinavian Thermometer

(Always tree below zero)

Hopkins still celebrates its title of "Raspberry Capital of the United States" in an annual raspberry festival. The area no longer produces the quantities of raspberries it once did, since most of this prime land has been developed for other purposes. But residents of Hopkins still know how to appreciate the seedy little berry that brought them fame.

Raspberry Yogurt Dessert
"a healthy treat"

2 **egg whites, stiffly beaten**
½ **cup whipping cream, whipped**
2 **tablespoons rum**
2 **cups red raspberry yogurt**
1 **cup grated coconut**
2 **tablespoons grated orange peel**

Combine all ingredients until well mixed. Refrigerate until set.

4 to 6 servings

The Northern Lights, or Aurora Borealis, are a breathtaking, unforgettable phenomenon which sometimes grace the Minnesota skies. These meteoric streamers of light across the northern heavens make the sky seem to be on fire with strokes of colorful liquid light, whisked across the firmament by a giant celestial brush. "Aurora" was the goddess of the dawn, from the same Latin root as "to burn" and "gold." You can capture some of the thrill of the Northern Lights with this spectacular flaming dessert.

Flaming Bananas
"a tableside production with style"

- 2 tablespoons butter
- ⅓ cup sugar
- ½ cup orange juice
- 2 tablespoons orange liqueur
- 4 bananas, sliced crosswise or lengthwise in half
- ¼ cup brandy

In a chafing dish, melt butter. Add sugar, stirring constantly, until liquified (caramelized). When mixed together thoroughly, add orange juice and liqueur. Add sliced bananas. When they are warm, pour on the brandy (no need to warm it) and light carefully. Enjoy the spectacle.

4 servings

**"Ye who love a nation's legend . . .
Love the ballads of a people,
Listen to this Indian Legend."**

These poetic lines herald the annual "Song of Hiawatha" pageant performed in Pipestone by 200 local people. Also famous for the quarries of stone prized for peace pipes, this area is now a sacred neutral ground for many tribes of Indians. It became a National Monument in 1937, one of two in Minnesota. This refreshing dessert will be so popular, you'd better pipe up for a piece.

Lemon Legend Dessert
"a sure bet for summer"

Vanilla wafers or
graham crackers
1 (14-ounce) can
sweetened condensed
milk
3 eggs, lightly beaten
2 medium lemons
1 cup whipping cream,
whipped

Place cookies or crackers on bottom of 13x9x2-inch pan. Add sweetened condensed milk to eggs. Add the juice (about 4 to 6 tablespoons) and grated peel (about 2 tablespoons) of the lemons; beat until smooth. Fold in whipped cream. Pour mixture over cookies. Freeze 2 hours.

15 servings

"Icebox of the Nation" is the dubious honor bestowed on Minnesota by virtue of its frigid winters. These winters are often so cold that spoken words freeze in the air and fall to the ground in layers. Then with the thaw, this defrosted dialogue creates a conversational roar that can be heard in Chicago. Also frozen in layers, this delicious dessert captures the harmonious concerto of ice cream, chocolate and nuts — great in any season.

Arctic Parfait
"freeze your cookies"

1 (16-ounce) package Oreo cookies, crushed
½ cup butter, melted
½ gallon vanilla ice cream
1½ cups Spanish peanuts
Fudge Topping:
½ cup butter or margarine
2 cups powdered sugar
1 (12-ounce) can evaporated milk
⅔ cup chocolate chips
1 teaspoon vanilla

Mix crushed cookies and butter together; press into 13x9x2-inch pan. Refrigerate. Slice ice cream and place over crust. Sprinkle peanuts over ice cream; place in freezer. Combine topping ingredients in a saucepan. Heat until chips melt; boil over low heat 8 minutes, stirring constantly. Cool and spread over ice cream and nuts. Return to freezer. Freeze at least 2 hours. Remove from freezer 15 minutes before serving.

18 servings

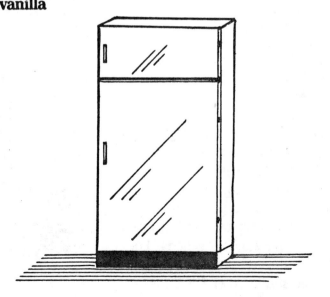

A tree that has evoked both fear and reverence through the ages is the Witch Tree on Hat Point near Grand Portage. This twisted and gnarled 300-year-old cedar, clutching menacingly to the rocky cliff overlooking Lake Superior, cast a spell over Indians and Voyageurs who dared to venture near it. Believed to contain an evil spirit in the shape of a bird, it was quite capable of capsizing even a 36-foot canoe on a wicked whim. Brave travelers would present the tree with treasured gifts in hopes of securing safe passage. It is clear that this was no tree to trifle with.

Banana Trifle
"a bewitching dessert"

1 (3-ounce) package strawberry-flavor gelatin
¾ cup boiling water
Ice cubes
½ cup cold water
1 cup sliced bananas
1 cup sliced strawberries
2 cups ½-inch pound cake cubes
¼ cup orange juice
1 (4-serving size) instant vanilla pudding/pie mix
1½ cups cold milk
½ cup frozen whipped topping, thawed

Dissolve gelatin in boiling water. Add ice cubes to cold water to make 1¼ cups; add to gelatin, stirring until slightly thickened. Remove unmelted ice. Stir in bananas and strawberries. Place cake cubes in large serving or trifle bowl; sprinkle with orange juice. Spoon gelatin mixture over cake. Chill 15 minutes. Prepare pudding mix with milk according to package directions. Let stand a few minutes to thicken; fold in whipped topping. Spoon over gelatin in bowl. Chill.

10 servings

On February 24, 1985, thousands of people gathered to watch the spectacular burst as St. Paul's vintage 1889 High Bridge was dynamited into eternity. It certainly brought a nostalgic lump to many a throat to witness the demise of this unique and familar old span across the Mississippi River. Of course, time and progress take their toll, and the old must often make way for the new. But not always, and here is a 1905 pudding recipe to prove it. A real blast from the past!

Old-Fashioned Chocolate Steamed Pudding
"bridges the decades"

1 cup all-purpose flour
½ cup sugar
½ cup milk
1 egg, well beaten
1 tablespoon butter
½ teaspoon salt
1 teaspoon cream of tartar
1 (1-ounce) square unsweetened chocolate, melted and cooled

Combine all ingredients; place in small covered tin and steam 45 minutes. Remove from tin and serve warm or cool with Hard Sauce.

4 to 6 servings

Hard Sauce

1 cup powdered sugar
½ cup butter, softened
1 egg, beaten
⅛ teaspoon vanilla

Cream powdered sugar and butter in small mixer bowl until well blended and fluffy. Blend in egg and vanilla until smooth.

Makes about 1 cup

Maud Hart Lovelace is known and loved for her *Betsy-Tacy* books. Born in Mankato, she based many of these delightful stories on her childhood. One delicious afternoon, Betsy, Tacy and Tib decide to make an "Everything Pudding," using a little bit of everything they can find in the kitchen: a little bacon grease, a little milk, a little flour . . . tapioca, cinnamon, pepper, chocolate, vinegar, oil, onion . . . Ohhh. Needless to say, after eating it they didn't feel so good. This dessert is not quite as creative as theirs, but it will leave you feeling just fine.

Pudding Dessert
"everything nice"

Crust:
1 cup flour
½ cup margarine, melted
½ cup finely chopped nuts
Filling:
1 (8-ounce) package
cream cheese, softened
1 cup powdered sugar
1 cup frozen whipped
topping, thawed
2 (4-serving) packages
any flavor instant
pudding mix
3 cups milk
Topping:
1 cup frozen whipped
topping, thawed
½ cup finely chopped nuts

Heat oven to 350°. Combine flour, margarine and nuts. Pat on bottom of greased 13x9x2-inch pan. Bake 20 minutes; cool. Blend cream cheese, powdered sugar and whipped topping; spread on crust. Beat pudding and milk together; pour over cream cheese layer. Spread with remaining whipped topping; sprinkle with remaining nuts. Refrigerate.

15 servings

Hint: Use 1 package butterscotch and 1 package vanilla pudding, or use 1 package chocolate and 1 package vanilla pudding, or use 2 packages pistachio pudding.

All Minnesotans know of the distinct, unique, rare, individual and delicate beauty possessed by each and every snow flake. Like human thumbprints, no two are alike. Sometimes it helps to reflect on this minute yet infinite artistry as we watch those little frozen masterpieces of symmetry accumulating on our driveways in depths of over 3 feet, with drifts of over 6 feet. With our shovels and snowblowers, we are certainly insensitive to the joy of it all. Minnesota children, however, often keep sight of the wonder of the snowflake, occasionally capturing a solitary one to savor on the tongue or to contemplate on the mitten. And in masses, it's rapture! Snowmen, snow forts, snowball fights, cut-the-pie, angels-in-the-snow, sledding, sliding and other fun possibilities, as limitless as the imagination.

Snowflake Pudding

1 cup sugar
1 envelope unflavored gelatin
½ teaspoon salt
1¼ cup milk
1 teaspoon vanilla
1 (3½-ounce) can coconut
2 cups whipping cream, whipped

Thoroughly mix sugar, gelatin and salt; add milk and stir over medium heat until gelatin mixture is dissolved. Chill until partially set (mixture will separate). Add vanilla; then fold in coconut and whipped cream. Pile into 1½-quart mold. Refrigerate until firm, about 4 hours or longer. Serve with raspberries or strawberries, if desired.

8 servings

187

Minnesotans love to set records. The largest kazoo band in history orchestrated a 1980 Kicks game and made the *Guinness Book of World Records.* On October 12, 1981, the world's largest marching band, thundering with 3006 pairs of boots, marched in Minneapolis. In 1979, the opening of the Hennepin Center for the Arts was regaled by a choreographed assemblage of tap dancers, who hop-shuffle-stepped their way down Hennepin Avenue and into star-spangled history.

Tap Tap-ioca
"a refreshing rhythm for the dessert records"

¼ cup tapioca
1½ cups sugar
½ teaspoon salt
2½ cups cut-up rhubarb
2½ cups water
1 (8-ounce) can crushed
   pineapple

Combine all ingredients except pineapple. Cook mixture until it boils; cool. Add undrained pineapple. Serve with whipped cream, if desired.

4 servings

On the Banks of the Plum Creek is Laura Ingalls Wilder's fourth and most widely read book of the popular "Little House" series. These stories are set in Walnut Grove, where the Ingalls family lived in the 1870's. The long-running television series "Little House on the Prairie" put Walnut Grove in the national spotlight.

Plum Creek Plum Pudding
"plumb yummy"

1½ cups graham flour
 1 cup raisins
 1 cup currants
 1 cup milk
 ½ cup molasses
 1 teaspoon soda
 1 tablespoon hot water
 3 tablespoons sugar
 3 tablespoons butter, melted
 Brown Sugar Sauce:
1½ cups packed brown sugar
 2 tablespoons cornstarch
 1 teaspoon nutmeg
 Butter
 Salt
 1 cup boiling water
 Vinegar or rum to taste

Combine all pudding ingredients; mix well. Pour into greased 4-cup covered mold (or cover with aluminum foil); steam over boiling water 2 hours. For Sauce, mix all ingredients together. Serve over pudding.

6 to 8 servings

The Smoky Hills area near Park Rapids was so named by the Indians because of the blue haze which hovers over the hills in the summertime. This haze is a mantle of humidity created by the breath of the trees as it meets the prairie air. Indians had a portage-free route by canoe from Fort Snelling via the Mississippi and Crow Wing Rivers to the Shell River, ending up in their beloved Smoky Hills.

Village Bread Pudding

4 cups soft bread crumbs
2 cups milk
¼ cup butter
½ cup sugar
2 eggs, slightly beaten
¼ teaspoon salt
1 teaspoon vanilla, optional
1 teaspoon cinnamon or nutmeg
½ cup raisins
  Hard Sauce (page 185) or cream, optional

Place bread crumbs in 1½-quart baking dish. Scald milk with butter. Blend milk and remaining ingredients into bread crumbs. Place baking dish in pan of hot water (1 inch deep). Bake at 350° for 40 to 45 minutes or until knife inserted 1 inch from edge comes out clean. Serve warm with Hard Sauce or cream.

4 servings

Yum yum yum. Minnesotans love to eat, and they love to party; hence the happy coupling of food and festivals. If you adore peanut butter and milk, go to Litchfield. The Minnesota Sit and Spit Club in Motley has found that cherry pits make great ammunition. Sauerkraut Days in Henderson, Muskie Days in Nevis, a smelt fry in Beaver Bay, wild rice festivals at Kelliher on the Upper Red Lake, and more and more. Wherever you may be going, they'll be eating something and celebrating it — you can depend on that.

Wild Rice Pudding
"a festival of flavor"

1½ cups cooked wild rice
¼ teaspoon salt
2 cups milk, scalded
⅓ cup sugar
2 eggs, well beaten
1 teaspoon vanilla

Heat oven to 325°. Combine all ingredients in buttered 1½-quart casserole or deep dish. Bake 25 to 30 minutes or until set.

4 servings

St. Paul's skyline silhouettes not one but two famous domes: St. Paul's Cathedral and the State Capitol, which boasts the world's largest unsupported dome. The capitol's design was chosen in a contest, won by Cass Gilbert, a native Minnesota architect. "Prosperity," a gilded copper statue in a chariot pulled by four horses, surveys the surroundings from atop the capitol. On the 4th of July, those surroundings are obscured with the throngs of people who turn out to enjoy a gigantic picnic called "Taste of Minnesota," featuring edibles by scores of local restaurants. This event and our beautiful capitol are both as American as apple pie bars.

Apple Pie Bars

Crust:
2 cups all-purpose flour
1 teaspoon salt
⅔ cup shortening
1 egg yolk, beaten
½ cup milk
Filling:
6 medium apples, peeled and sliced
½ to ¾ cup sugar
1 teaspoon cinnamon
1 teaspoon nutmeg
Glaze:
¾ cup powdered sugar
1 to 1½ tablespoons water

Heat oven to 350°. Mix crust ingredients together. Roll out half of crust to fit 13x9x2-inch pan. Place in pan and press out to fit. Combine filling ingredients; put over crust in pan. Roll out top crust; place over apples. Bake about 50 minutes until top crust is golden brown. Combine powdered sugar and enough water to make a smooth glaze. While bars are warm, drizzle with glaze.

Makes 3 dozen

Why is the capital of Minnesota in St. Paul and not in St. Peter? In 1857 there was a bill before the legislature which would probably have effected such a move were it not for the flamboyant territorial legislator, Joe Rolette. Decked out in full voyageur-trader costume, he usually arrived dramatically in St. Paul on his bell-spangled dogsled to begin each session. He did not appear at the session in question, however, but stole the bill and hid in the attic of a local hotel until moments before the closing of the session. This rather unorthodox and broadly-cursed tactic served its purpose well, for our capital remains yet in St. Paul.

Audacious Lemon Bars

2 cups all-purpose flour
1 cup butter, softened
½ cup powdered sugar
4 eggs
2 cups granulated sugar
3 tablespoons flour
2 medium lemons
1 teaspoon baking
  powder

Mix flour, butter and powdered sugar together as for pie crust. Spread in 13x9x2-inch pan. Bake about 20 minutes. While baking, beat eggs with granulated sugar, flour, juice and peel of lemons. Just before pouring into crust, stir in baking powder. Bake 20 minutes longer, until set. Cool; cut into bars.

Makes 2 dozen

The building of the railroads created instant competition for river transportation. A true riverman would spit a curse on each railroad track he crossed — possibly a case of "sour grapes," for which we would recommend the following cure:

Sour Cream Raisin Bars

Crust:
- 1¾ cups all-purpose flour
- 1¾ cups rolled oats
- 1 cup packed brown sugar
- 1 cup butter, softened
- 1 teaspoon baking soda

Filling:
- 4 egg yolks, beaten
- 1¾ cups dairy sour cream
- 2 cups raisins
- ¼ cup half and half
- 1¼ cups sugar
- 3 tablespoons cornstarch
- 1 teaspoon cinnamon
- ½ teaspoon nutmeg
- ¼ teaspoon ground cloves

Heat oven to 350°. Combine crust ingredients; press ⅔ of mixture on bottom of 13x9x2-inch pan. Mix filling ingredients in saucepan and heat over medium heat, stirring constantly, until thick. Pour over crust. Sprinkle with reserved topping mixture. Bake 30 minutes or until golden brown. Cool; cut into bars.

Makes 4 dozen

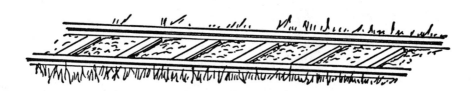

Peter, Peter, Pumpkin Eater's wife could have had a nine-bedroom estate in the pumpkin which won the Blue Ribbon at the 1982 State Fair. That horticultural marvel weighed in at 184 pounds, unfurnished. Our state fair is also one of the largest and best in the country, with primarily an agricultural focus. It always offers plenty of variety, though, including big-name entertainment and a full-blown Midway. You can get all the milk you can drink at the dairy booth to complement these prize pumpkin bars.

Pumpkin Bars
"blue ribbon"

2 cups all-purpose flour
2 teaspoons baking powder
½ teaspoon salt
1 teaspoon pumpkin pie spice
1 teaspoon cinnamon
1 teaspoon baking soda
4 eggs
1 (16-ounce) can pumpkin
2 cups sugar
1 cup vegetable oil
1 cup chopped nuts
Frosting:
1 (3-ounce) package cream cheese, softened
1 tablespoon milk
1¾ cups powdered sugar
¾ cup margarine or butter, softened
1 teaspoon vanilla

Heat oven to 350°. Combine dry ingredients. Add eggs, pumpkin, sugar and oil; beat well. Stir in nuts. Spread in greased 15x10x1-inch pan. Bake about 25 minutes. Cool. For frosting, combine all ingredients; blend well. Spread on bars.

Makes about 2½ dozen

Over 60 "fancy houses" bestudded St. Paul from the 1860's to the 1920's, but the fanciest, most luxurious and most prominent was that of Nina Clifford, the last of the great madams. She reigned as the legendary queen of the not-so-saintly St. Paul, catering to a cultured, powerful and elite clientele. Nina's brownstone in the old Hill Street area was the setting for many business and political decisions that affected the future of St. Paul, and it is said that her loans kept several distinguished businessmen from bankruptcy. When she died, all the leading business and civic leaders of the city were called, as a joke, and informed that she had named them in her will to be her pallbearer. On the day of her funeral, the conspicuous exodus from town of vast numbers of noteworthy men served as a final tribute to her widespread influence.

Fancy Caramel Oatmeal Bars
"decadent"

64 caramels
½ cup plus 2 tablespoons milk
2 cups rolled oats
2 cups all-purpose flour
1½ cups packed brown sugar
1 teaspoon baking soda
1 teaspoon salt
1½ cups margarine, softened
2 cups chocolate chips
1 cup chopped pecans

Melt caramels in milk; set aside to cool slightly. Heat oven to 350°. Mix oats, flour, brown sugar, soda, salt and margarine together. Press half of mixture into 15x10x1-inch pan. Bake 10 minutes. Sprinkle chocolate chips and nuts evenly over baked crust. Drizzle with caramel mixture; top with remaining crust mixture. Bake 10 to 15 minutes longer.

Makes 5 dozen

Joe and Josie Ruttgers homesteaded on Bay Lake in the 1880's. A perfect site for camping and fishing, their beautiful lakeside land became very popular with visitors, and the genial "Grandma" Ruttgers would feed them and play the piano. After World War I a few cottages sprang up, and the hospitality provided by the Ruttgers, along with the natural air-conditioning provided by the lake, created a very lively summer environment. Soon Ruttgers' on Bay Lake became known as the first resort in Minnesota. Brownies were always a big hit among the guests.

First Resort Brownies
"a chocolate lover's favorite option"

½ cup margarine, softened
1 cup sugar
4 eggs
1 teaspoon vanilla
Pinch of salt
1 (16-ounce) can chocolate syrup
1 cup plus 1 tablespoon all-purpose flour
½ cup chopped walnuts
Frosting:
2 cups sugar
2 tablespoons unsweetened cocoa powder
¼ cup light corn syrup
½ cup milk
½ cup margarine, butter or shortening
¼ teaspoon salt
3 large marshmallows
1 teaspoon vanilla

Lightly grease and flour 13x9x2-inch pan. Heat oven to 350°. Blend all brownie ingredients together; beat in eggs one at a time. Bake 25 to 30 minutes; cool. For frosting, combine all ingredients except marshmallows and vanilla in saucepan. Stir over low heat until margarine melts. Bring to a full rolling boil, stirring constantly. Boil 1 minute; remove from heat. Add marshmallows; beat until lukewarm. Stir in vanilla; continue beating until smooth spreading consistency. Spread on brownies; cut into bars.

Makes 4 dozen

Weather is a popular topic of conversation in Minnesota, and rightly so, for it is decidedly fascinating here, and a more varied climate cannot be found. Winters in particular are the source of innumerable jokes, stories and riddles, as mesmerized Minnesotans become obsessed with the numerical reckoning of snowfall inches, windchill factors and degree days. The mere mention of a wind chill temperature of 50° or 80° or even 100° *below* zero is enough to immobilize even the most stoic among us, and keep even the hardiest housebound. As these conditions persist, "cabin fever" becomes a reality.

Blizzard Bars
"to help cure cabin fever"

1 cup butter, softened
1 cup packed brown
  sugar
½ cup granulated sugar
4 cups rolled oats
1 teaspoon vanilla
  Frosting:
1 (6-ounce) package
  chocolate chips
¾ cup peanut butter
1 teaspoon vanilla

Heat oven to 350°. Mix all bar ingredients until crumbly; press into 15x10x1-inch pan. Bake 10 to 12 minutes; cool. Heat frosting ingredients in double boiler over hot water until chips are melted. Spread over bars; cut into squares.

Makes 5 dozen

Charles Schultz, originator of the "Peanuts" comic strip, is from St. Paul. Some other famous people who hail from Minnesota are Charlton Heston, Pinky Lee, Jane Russell, Robert Preston, the Andrews sisters, Jessica Lange, Loni Anderson and Guindon.

Salted "Peanuts" Bars

3 cups all-purpose flour
1½ cups packed brown sugar
1 cup butter, softened
¼ teaspoon salt
1 (12-ounce) package butterscotch chips
½ cup light corn syrup
3 tablespoons butter
3 tablespoons water
½ teaspoon vanilla
3 cups salted peanuts

Heat oven to 375°. Mix flour, brown sugar, butter and salt together; pat into greased 15x10x1-inch pan. Bake 10 minutes. In saucepan, heat chips, syrup, butter and water together until chips are melted. Stir in vanilla and peanuts; spread immediately over crust. Bake 8 minutes longer. Cool slightly; cut into bars while still warm.

Makes 5 dozen

Frozen lakes and skating rinks set the stage for a favorite Minnesota sport, hockey. From Mites, Peewees, and Midgets to the Gophers and the North Stars, it draws a huge following of enthusiastic fans. In fact, Eveleth is the site of the U.S. Hockey Hall of Fame, where the sport and its elite are immortalized. The North Stars played in the 1981 and the 1991 Stanley Cup Finals. A former Gopher and North Star coach, Herb Brooks of St. Paul, coached the U.S. Olympic team that packed the puck to an improbable victory in 1980. This Gold Medal team was more than half comprised of Minnesotans. Not all of our ice skills are long-blade, either. We also cut a fine figure on ice and, in evidence, Duluth is the birthplace of the famous Ice Capades.

Iced Sheet Cookies
"real sliders"

1 cup raisins
½ cup butter, softened
½ cup shortening
1½ cups sugar
2 eggs, beaten
3 cups all-purpose flour
1½ teaspoons baking soda
1 teaspoon ground cloves
1 teaspoon salt
1 cup chopped nuts
Frosting:
2 cups powdered sugar
   Grated orange peel
   Water

Heat oven to 375°. Boil raisins 5 minutes with enough water to make 1 cup raisin liquid; cool. Cream butter, shortening and sugar; add eggs. Mix in dry ingredients, raisins, raisin juice and nuts. Spread in two greased 15x10x1-inch pans. Bake 15 minutes. For frosting, mix powdered sugar with orange peel and enough water to make a thick frosting. Spread on warm bars. Cool; cut into squares.

Makes 8 to 10 dozen

The creative artistry of Minnesota's winters is nowhere more dramatically visible than in the fanciful ice sculptures and formations created when the suspended waves and spray freeze on the rocky shores of Lake Superior. Another sight which is impressive for fantastic shapes as well as for sheer mass is the spring ice break-up on Lake Mille Lacs, when thousands of tons of ice amass on the shores, making a great show of the ending of winter.

Icebox Cookies
"buttery delights which know no season"

2 cups butter, softened
2 eggs
3½ cups all-purpose flour
2 cups sugar
3 teaspoons baking powder
1 teaspoon vanilla
1 cup chopped nuts
1 (1-ounce) square unsweetened chocolate
½ tablespoon butter

Cream 2 cups butter; add eggs and beat. Stir dry ingredients together; add to butter and egg mixture. Blend in vanilla and nuts. Divide dough in half. Melt chocolate and ½ tablespoon butter together; add to half of the dough. Shape into rolls; refrigerate overnight. Heat oven to 350°. Cut dough into thin slices. Bake 10 to 12 minutes.

Makes 7 to 8 dozen

In 1913, the Hupmobile was a vehicle that everyone was excited about, but nobody wanted to buy. So "Bus Andy" Anderson and Carl Wickman decided to charge a lot of people just a little to ride in it. When iron ore was found under Hibbing, the entire town was moved 2 miles. They posted a sign reading "Hibbing to Alice, 15¢ one way, 25¢ Round Trip." It immediately became popular, taking men to the mines in the morning and home in the evening. Their venture eventually grew into the prominent Greyhound Bus Lines, one of the largest in the world, and Hibbing became known as the "Birthplace of Bus Transportation." When touring our enterprising and captivating state via Hupmobile or auto, be sure to enjoy the scenery and munch on some of these snappy snacks.

Crunchy Round-Trip Cookies
"still just as crisp on the way home"

1 cup granulated sugar
1 cup packed brown sugar
1 cup margarine, softened
1 cup vegetable oil
2 eggs
1 teaspoon vanilla
3½ cups all-purpose flour
1 teaspoon cream of tartar
1 teaspoon baking soda
1 teaspoon salt
½ cup chopped nuts
1 cup flaked or shredded coconut
1 cup rolled oats
1 cup Rice Krispies

Blend sugars, margarine, oil, eggs and vanilla. In separate bowl, stir dry ingredients together; add to first mixture and blend well. Stir in nuts, coconut, oats and cereal. Chill dough. Heat oven to 350°. Drop by teaspoonfuls onto ungreased cookie sheets. Press down with a fork until very thin. If dough is sticky, chill fork in ice water and wipe dry. Bake 10 to 12 minutes.

Makes 7 dozen

Sugar Cookies
"like Grandma used to make"

3 eggs
1 cup shortening
1 cup sugar
1 teaspoon vanilla
3 cups all-purpose flour
2 teaspoons cream of
  tartar
1 teaspoon baking soda
1 teaspoon salt

Heat oven to 350°. Beat eggs until light. Cream shortening and sugar well. Add eggs and blend. Blend in vanilla and dry ingredients. Roll dough out thin and cut into desired shapes. Decorate before or after baking. Bake about 8 minutes.

Makes 5 dozen

Note: Dough can also be shaped into balls and flattened slightly with a glass dipped in sugar. Baked cookies can be frosted with a glaze.

Chewy Macaroons
"lo-cal delight"

1 tablespoon flour
½ cup sugar
¼ teaspoon salt
2 egg whites, at room
  temperature
½ teaspoon vanilla
2 cups flaked coconut
24 candied cherries (or
  well-drained
  maraschino cherries)

Heat oven to 325°. Lightly grease and flour 2 large cookie sheets. Combine flour, sugar and salt. In separate large mixer bowl, beat egg whites until stiff but not dry. Beat in vanilla; fold in dry ingredients and coconut. Drop by rounded teaspoonful about 2 inches apart on cookie sheets. Press cherry into center of each. Bake 12 to 20 minutes, until pale golden brown.

Makes 2 dozen (55 calories each)

No-Bake Cookies
"thrill your guests"

2 cups sugar
½ cup margarine
½ cup milk
¼ cup unsweetened cocoa
  powder
1 teaspoon vanilla
⅔ cup peanut butter
2 cups rolled oats

Combine sugar, margarine, milk and cocoa in medium saucepan. Bring to a boil; boil 2 minutes, stirring often. Remove from heat and immediately stir in vanilla, peanut butter and oats; mix thoroughly. Drop by teaspoonfuls onto waxed paper. Refrigerate until firm.

Makes 3 to 4 dozen

Glensheen is the 7.6 acre estate in Duluth built by Chester and Clara Congdon on the western shore of Lake Superior between 1905 and 1908. It has been operated by the University of Minnesota as a historic site since 1979. A visitor to the estate steps back in time to experience the bygone lifestyle from the turn of the century. The Docent Council of Glensheen has compiled a collection of recipes that were served during the Congdon family days. In these handwritten files, some of the dishes had notes by members of the Congdon family; this recipe was marked "Good."

Rocks

⅔ cup butter
1¼ cups sugar
2 eggs, beaten
1 teaspoon cinnamon
1 teaspoon cloves
1 tablespoon melted
   unsweetened chocolate
2 cups all-purpose flour
1½ cups nuts
1½ cups raisins
1 teaspoon baking soda,
   dissolved in a little
   warm water

Cream butter and sugar. Add the eggs. Add cinnamon, cloves, chocolate and flour. Add this mixture to butter and egg mixture. Then add nuts, raisins and baking soda. If desired, add brandy or sherry flavoring. Drop from spoon on greased tins and bake at 350° until golden.

Makes 5 to 6 dozen

The Science Museum of Minnesota in St. Paul provides a unique "hands-on" experience for visitors of all ages. Combining science with natural history, its unique approach includes demonstrations, dramatic presentations and exhibits in which the viewer participates. Probably the greatest highlight is the spectacular, space-age William L. McKnight Omnitheater, built in 1978. The 76-foot domed screen and ultra-sophisticated projection and sound system can carry you into a volcano, swimming through coral reefs, running the Colorado River rapids or soaring precariously among mountain cliffs. The sights and sounds totally surround you and sweep your senses into vicarious thrills and unforgettable adventures.

Hands-on Cashew Brittle
"try to resist it"

2 cups sugar
1 cup light corn syrup
½ cup water
1 cup butter
3 cups (12 ounces) cashews
1 teaspoon baking soda

In a 3-quart saucepan, combine sugar, syrup and water; cook and stir until sugar dissolves. Bring to a boil and blend in butter. Stir frequently after mixture reaches thread stage (230°). Add cashews when mixture reaches 280° and stir constantly until it reaches hard crack stage (300°). Remove from heat; quickly stir in soda, mixing thoroughly. Quickly pour onto 2 buttered cookie sheets and spread around. Stretch out with forks. As it cools, pull on ends to stretch it thin. Loosen; turn over and break when cool.

Makes 2½ to 3 pounds

Minnesota is, in a manner of speaking, the belly button of the North American Continent. We are the geographic center as measured from east to west across the United States, and from the northern tip to the southern toe of the continent. These little chocolate candies will bring continental contentment to the geographic center of your body.

Chocolate Belly Buttons

2 pounds milk chocolate
   chunks
1 cup whipping cream,
   whipped
1 (5-ounce) package
   walnuts or pecans,
   crushed

Melt chocolate; cool but do not let reset. Stir in whipped cream; cool until workable. Butter hands; shape chocolate into small balls. Roll balls in crushed nuts; place on waxed paper to cool completely.

Makes about 2½ pounds

Festival Land Snacks
and Beverages

Francis Johnson of Darwin made it into the *Guinness Book of World Records* in 1974 for a ball of twine which he started to roll in 1950. In 1981 it was 40 feet in circumference, over 13 feet in diameter and it tipped the scales at 21,140 pounds. Of course, this tonnage was somewhat inflated since the stringish sphere had been rained on and was soaking wet. Nevertheless, as far as we know, Mr. Johnson's amazing orb remains uncontested as "the largest ball of twine in the world."

Salmon Party Ball
"sets records as world's fastest shrinking ball"

1 (16-ounce) can red or pink salmon
1 (8-ounce) package cream cheese, softened
1 tablespoon lemon juice
2 teaspoons grated onion
1 teaspoon prepared horseradish
¼ teaspoon salt
⅛ to ¼ teaspoon liquid smoke
½ cup chopped pecans
3 tablespoons snipped parsley

Drain and flake salmon. Combine with cream cheese, lemon juice, onion, horseradish, salt and liquid smoke. Shape into a ball; chill several hours. Combine pecans and parsley; roll salmon ball in mixture. Chill well. Serve with assorted crackers.

10 to 12 servings

Nutty Cheese Ball

2 (8-ounce) packages
  cream cheese, softened
1 cup butter, softened
¼ to ½ teaspoon garlic
  powder
½ cup Spanish peanuts,
  with skins, crushed

Blend cream cheese and butter together. Add garlic powder to taste. Shape into a ball and roll in peanuts; refrigerate. Serve with crackers.

12 to 15 servings

Fruity Cheese Ball

2 (8-ounce) packages
  cream cheese, softened
¼ cup finely chopped
  green pepper
2 tablespoons finely
  chopped onion
1 (8-ounce) can crushed
  pineapple, well drained
1 teaspoon seasoned salt
Chopped walnuts or
pecans

Combine all ingredients except nuts; shape into a ball. Refrigerate until firm. Roll in nuts. Serve with crackers.

12 to 15 servings

Olive Cheese Ball

2 (8-ounce) packages
  cream cheese, softened
2 ounces blue cheese
8 ounces Cheddar cheese,
  shredded (about 2 cups)
3 dashes of cayenne
  pepper
½ teaspoon garlic salt
½ teaspoon seasoned salt
1 teaspoon
  Worcestershire sauce
½ cup chopped green
  olives
¾ cup chopped ripe olives
Sliced olives

Combine cheeses and seasonings; mix in chopped olives. Line a medium bowl with foil and fill with cheese mixture. Chill thoroughly. Shape into 2 balls; decorate with sliced olives. Serve with snack crackers.

25 to 30 servings

The very first printed words about Paul Bunyan originated in Akeley as part of the national publicity campaign for the Red River Lumber Company, owned by J. B. Walker and his partner, Mr. Akeley. These two lumber barons left enduring marks on our state. J. B. Walker is the founder of the Walker Art Center as well as the town of Walker, where his partner Akeley lived. Incidentally, Mr. Walker named his town Akeley. At the time of the Paul Bunyan promotion, theirs was the largest privately owned sawmill in the world, shipping 20 to 30 freightcars of lumber a day via the Great Northern Railway. Once chronicled in print, Paul's renown quickly carpeted the nation, making Akeley famous as his "birthplace." The town still has his cradle to prove it.

Curried Cheese Log
"a success story"

2 **pounds sharp Cheddar cheese**
6 **ounces cream cheese, softened**
2 **cloves garlic, chopped**
  Cayenne pepper to taste
2 **cups chopped pecans**
  Curry powder to taste

Put cheeses, garlic and cayenne through a grinder or food processor alternately; mix thoroughly. Add nuts. Shape into 4 cylinders; roll in curry powder and wrap in plastic wrap. Refrigerate 24 hours or up to 1 week. Serve with crackers.

18 to 20 servings

The swarthy, dashing Indian-French Bois Brules, dressed in blue clothes with brass buttons, red sashes and beaded caps and mocassins, were the overland version of the voyageurs. These drivers of the Red River oxcarts hauled furs and buffalo hides from Moorhead, Roseau and other points northwest, often meeting in St. Cloud on their way to the steamboat landings in St. Paul. The racket from the 6-foot wooden wheels could be heard for many miles. When you travel Highway 10 or Highway 94 today, you are following old ox-cart trails — it took them a month to make a round trip we now make in a day. The drivers of the ox-carts chewed pemmican, dried buffalo or dried beef. But it's doubtful that theirs ever received such creative treatment as this.

Beefy-Olive Spread

2 cups shredded Cheddar
   cheese (about 8 ounces)
1 cup chopped ripe olives
½ cup chopped onion
1 (4-ounce) package
   smoked beef, cut up
1 teaspoon curry powder

Combine all ingredients. Serve with Rye Krisp or English muffins, cut into sixths.

Makes about 1½ cups

Currently under the flashing baton of conductor Edo deWaart, the world-class Minnesota Orchestra resonates in the architecturally intriguing Orchestra Hall in downtown Minneapolis. Not to be outshone, St. Paul's shimmering Ordway Music Theatre resounds with performances by the St. Paul Chamber Orchestra, the Schubert Club and the Minnesota Opera Company. Since 1987 the St. Paul Chamber Orchestra has innovatively operated under the direction of a 3-person artistic leadership team. Like our pâté, these two Twin Cities cultural centers and their illustrious inhabitants are never passé.

Liver Pâté

½ pound chicken or young beef liver
½ cup butter, softened
2 tablespoons finely chopped onion
1 teaspoon dry mustard
1 teaspoon salt
⅛ teaspoon ground cloves
Pinch of cayenne pepper
Pinch of nutmeg

Place liver in saucepan; add enough water to barely cover. Bring to a boil; reduce heat and simmer 15 to 20 minutes. Drain liver; put through a fine food chopper or food processor. Combine remaining ingredients with liver and blend well.

Makes about 1 cup

A cherished find in Minnesota is the Lake Superior agate, chosen as the state stone in 1969. The bands of red, brown, gray and white make this hard and durable stone easy to identify and very prized. Even more unusal is thomsonite, found almost exclusively near Grand Marais in ancient outcrops of basalt. This gemstone has colorful concentric circles called "eyes." We think you'll see eye-to-eye with these two eye-pleasing appetizers.

Cheese-Artichoke Spread
"keep an eye on this one"

2 (14-ounce) cans artichoke hearts, drained
1 cup grated Parmesan cheese
1 cup mayonnaise
8 ounces Mozzarella cheese, shredded
Pinch of garlic salt
Parsley sprigs

Cut each artichoke heart into 6 to 8 pieces. Combine with remaining ingredients except parsley and spread in quiche or other flat pan. Bake at 350° for 25 to 30 minutes. Garnish with parsley; serve with wheat crackers.

8 to 10 servings

Thomsonite

Crabmeat Puffs
"and this one"

1 cup mayonnaise
2 egg whites, stiffly beaten
1 to 1½ cups flaked crabmeat
½ teaspoon salt
Toast or Melba toast rounds
Paprika

Fold mayonnaise into egg whites; gently stir in crabmeat and salt. Pile on toast rounds; sprinkle with paprika. Broil 3 minutes or until brown.

Makes 5 to 6 dozen

Calamities often give rise to great heroism, and the 1894 Hinckley fire was no exception. A railroad engineer named Jim Root saved 350 people by driving his train backwards through the conflagration, though his hand was burned to the throttle in the course of his courageous deed. The 1918 fire in St. Louis and Carlton Counties burned 8,000 square miles of forest and killed 453 people. Because of these two disastrous fires, the state passed Legislation to clean up slash left by logging companies. Forest fires remain a hazard in our well-wooded state, however. Another major fire occurred as recently as May of 1971, when 15,000 acres of timberland in Superior National Forest were ravaged in five days.

Blazin' Bean Dip
"adds a real spark to chips"

1 cup refried beans
1 teaspoon chopped
  jalapeño pepper
1 (8-ounce) carton dairy
  sour cream
2 green onions, chopped
¼ cup chopped ripe olives
  Shredded Cheddar
  cheese

Combine all ingredients except cheese; put in small greased casserole or baking dish. Sprinkle with cheese. Bake at 350° for about 25 minutes.

Makes about 2 cups

Horseradish Dip

1 cup mayonnaise
1 tablespoon prepared horseradish
1 tablespoon chili powder
1 teaspoon minced onion
1 teaspoon Worcestershire sauce

Combine all ingredients; mix well. Chill. Serve with raw vegetable sticks or slices.

Makes about 1 cup

Crunchy Dip

1 (10-ounce) package frozen chopped spinach, thawed
1 package Knorr dry vegetable soup mix
1 cup dairy sour cream
1 cup mayonnaise
1 (8-ounce) can water chestnuts, drained and chopped
2 green onions, finely chopped
1 (1-pound) round loaf unsliced sourdough bread

Drain spinach; squeeze dry; combine with remaining ingredients except bread. Refrigerate several hours to blend flavors. Cut top off bread; hollow out loaf. Save bread pieces to serve with dip. Fill hollow loaf with dip; serve surrounded with bread pieces, crackers and/or fresh vegetables.

Makes 2½ cups

Dill Dip

1 cup dairy sour cream
1 cup mayonnaise
1 teaspoon Beau Monde seasoning
1 teaspoon dried dill weed
1 teaspoon parsley flakes
1 teaspoon onion flakes

Combine all ingredients; blend well. Serve with fresh vegetables or crackers.

Makes 2 cups

The sky blackened and a noise like a roaring wind swept into Minnesota from the Dakotas on June 12, 1873. That was the first day of the locust invasion which plagued the state until 1877. Some described the noise as sounding like the jaws of hundreds of hogs as the insects chomped and devoured every living green leaf or bud in their path. The government offered $1.00 a bushel for the locusts, ironically making them a more valuable crop than wheat.

Bacon-Cheese Snacks
"could incite massive munching"

6 slices bacon, crisply
  fried and crumbled
¼ cup minced onion
½ teaspoon
  Worcestershire sauce
¼ teaspoon dry mustard
1 to 2 drops Tabasco
  sauce
6 ounces grated
  Parmesan cheese
4 ounces Cheddar or
  Swiss cheese, shredded
2 tablespoons mayonnaise
4 to 5 English muffins,
  split and toasted
⅛ teaspoon paprika

In a medium bowl, combine bacon and onion. Add Worcestershire sauce, mustard, Tabasco and Parmesan cheese; mix well. Add shredded cheese and mayonnaise; stir with fork. Spread mixture on muffins; sprinkle with paprika. Place in microwave on paper towel and microwave on medium for 2 to 3 minutes until cheese melts or broil in oven for 3 to 4 minutes until cheese melts. Quarter and serve.

Makes 16 to 20 snacks

The Aquatennial Festival is the largest civic festival in the United States, started in 1940 to revitalize Minneapolis after the Depression. Water activities, music, dance, art fairs and a parade still make splashy fun for the whole family. St. Paul hosts the Winter Carnival, started in 1886, and revived in 1916. The first ice palace was 106 feet high; now spectacular ice carving is done in Rice Park. Children love the tradition of the Vulcans, with their flamboyant capes and charcoaled faces, liberally bestowing sooty kisses on festival-goers. Also noteworthy is St. Paul's St. Patrick's Day Parade, once banned by the church, but restored to become the third largest in the country. After your favorite spectacle, enjoy this colorful pageant of flavors.

Taco Party Parade
"a new chip off the old guac"

1 (6-ounce) container
  frozen hot avocado dip,
  thawed
1 (8-ounce) package
  cream cheese, softened
1 (8-ounce) carton dairy
  sour cream
  Chopped tomatoes
  Chopped onions
  Chopped lettuce
  Chopped ripe olives
  Shredded Cheddar
  cheese

Blend avocado dip, cream cheese and sour cream. Spread mixture on serving plate and cover with vegetables and cheese. Serve with taco chips.

12 to 15 servings

If you find a buffalo head nickel, save it. They are rare now. The design was created by Minnesota sculptor James Earl Frazer of Winona, whose unique work also graces government buildings in Washington. Famous art from all over the world can be seen at the Minneapolis Institute of Arts, Walker Art Center and the Minnesota Museum of Art. The Minneapolis Sculpture Garden across from Walker, better known as "Cherry Stone Park," blossoms year-round with hardy 3-dimensional magnum opuses planted artfully among a maze of pathways.

Zucchini Appetizers
"artistic little bites"

3 cups thinly-sliced unpeeled zucchini (about 4 small)
1 cup biscuit mix
½ cup finely chopped onion
½ cup shredded cheese
2 tablespoons snipped parsley
½ teaspoon seasoned salt
½ teaspoon dried marjoram
1 clove garlic, finely chopped
½ cup vegetable oil
4 eggs, slightly beaten

Heat oven to 350°. Combine all ingredients and spread in greased 13x9x2-inch pan. Bake about 25 minutes or until golden brown. Cut into 2x1-inch pieces; serve warm. Can be frozen.

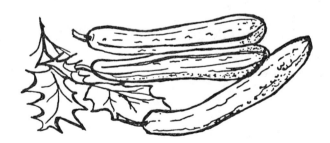

The newest and glitziest entity on the Minnesota sports scene is Minneapolis' Target Center, giving the Twin Cities more major arenas than any other metropolis in the country. Home of the NBA expansion Minnesota Timberwolves, its amenities include more bathrooms per capita than any other arena in the world. When you enter its neon-lit main entrance, the pulsating vibes of rap music propel you to escalators, which then whisk you to your seat location and to the endless array of food and souvenir vendors. Its restaurant and fitness center allow you to dine, exercise and watch a sporting event without ever going outside. But before working out, chowing down and looking on, try warming up with these delicious canapés.

Warm Quiche Lorraine Appetizers

Crust:
1½ packages pie crust mix (or recipe for 2-crust pie)
½ teaspoon dry mustard
1 teaspoon paprika
2 tablespoons butter, softened
Filling:
¾ pound bacon
1 cup chopped onion
3 cups shredded Swiss cheese (about 12 ounces)
6 eggs
4 cups light cream (or 1 pint half & half and 1 (12-ounce) can evaporated milk)
1½ teaspoons salt
1 teaspoon sugar
¼ teaspoon nutmeg
¼ teaspoon pepper
Dash of cayenne pepper

Prepare pie crust as directed on package or in recipe, adding seasonings to dry ingredients before adding liquid. Roll out to 18x15-inch rectangle; place crust in 10x15x1-inch pan. Flute edge. Spread with softened butter. Refrigerate until needed. Heat oven to 375°. Fry bacon until crisp; drain on paper towel, then crumble. Sauté onion in 2 tablespoons of the bacon drippings until golden. Sprinkle bacon over bottom of pastry shell. Sprinkle cheese over bacon. Sprinkle onion over cheese. In large bowl, beat eggs, cream and seasonings with rotary beater until well blended. Pour into shell. Bake 35 to 40 minutes until golden and firm. Let cool 10 minutes before cutting.

Makes 40 pieces

"They're neck in neck. . .and it's Pizza by a nose! Such jargon is commonplace in Minnesota since the June 1985 opening of Canterbury Downs in Shakopee. Queue up at the windows to place your pari-mutuel bets, and take our cue on this pizza recipe. It's a sure bet!

Finish Line Pizza
"in the winner's circle"

1 (8-ounce) package refrigerated crescent rolls
1 (8-ounce) package cream cheese, softened
⅓ cup mayonnaise
1 tablespoon dried dill weed
⅛ teaspoon garlic powder
1 tablespoon instant minced onion
Fresh mushrooms
Fresh carrots
Fresh broccoli
Fresh cauliflower
Ripe olives
Green pepper
Shredded Cheddar cheese

Heat oven to 375°. On ungreased 13 to 15-inch round pan, spread rolls to cover pan and seal edges together like pizza crust. Bake 5 to 10 minutes. Mix cream cheese, mayonnaise and seasonings; spread over crust. Cut vegetables into bite-size pieces; arrange in sections or mix randomly over cheese mix. Top with shredded cheese, gently pressing down. Chill 2 hours. Cut into small squares.

Makes 36 pieces

The strange and mysterious case of disappearing pigs near Harmony was serendipitously solved in 1926 when a farmer was out walking through his fields and heard their muted squeals and grunts. Following the sounds, he found not only his pigs, but also the opening to Niagara Cave, the largest of numerous caverns found in this section of Minnesota. It merits its name with a beautiful 60-foot waterfall some 200 feet underground. Other caves in the area are Mystery Cave near Spring Green and Yucatan Catacombs near Houston. The mushrooms which grow in many of these caves may have accounted for the strange disappearance of those pigs, but there will be no mystery in the way these toothsome hot mushrooms disappear!

Serendipity Mushrooms

"you'll be tempted to make a pig of yourself"

2 medium onions,
   chopped
½ cup butter
1 (8-ounce) package
   cream cheese, softened
1 pound fresh
   mushrooms, chopped
¼ teaspoon garlic salt
½ teaspoon
   Worcestershire sauce

Sauté chopped onions in butter; add to cream cheese and blend well. Add mushrooms, garlic salt and Worcestershire sauce; mix. Spoon into pie plate. Bake at 375° for 15 to 20 minutes. Serve hot on party rye bread. (This can be made ahead and heated just before serving.)

Makes about 3 cups

The morel only recently achieved official status as the state mushroom by a vote in the state legislature in 1984. This brown, spongy-topped treasure pops up in Minnesota forests and fields in the spring. If you have had the good fortune to pick a basket of these desirable mushrooms, you should be aware of the possibility of a distressing side effect called "morelitis," which results in a temporary loss of hearing when someone asks you where you found your morels.

Stuffed Mushrooms
"you stuff them, they'll stuff you"

24 (1½-inch) fresh
    mushrooms with stems
2 tablespoons butter
6 slices bacon
1 medium onion, finely
    chopped
2 tablespoons sherry
½ cup shredded
    Mozzarella cheese
¼ cup grated Parmesan
    cheese

Rinse mushrooms; remove stems and chop. Melt butter and coat bottom of 9x9x2-inch pan. Place mushroom caps, tops down, in pan. Put a dab of butter in each cap. Fry bacon; drain and crumble. Drain off all but 2 tablespoons of bacon drippings. Add onion and saute; stir in chopped mushroom stems, sherry and crumbled bacon; cook until sherry evaporates. Remove from heat; stir in Mozzarella cheese and 2 tablespoons Parmesan cheese. Spoon into mushroom caps; sprinkle with remaining Parmesan cheese. Bake about 10 minutes at 400°. Mushroom caps can be filled up to 24 hours in advance and refrigerated; bake 20 minutes.

Makes 2 dozen

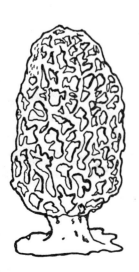

The first ore in Minnesota was discovered by "The Band of Brothers," otherwise known as the "7 Iron Men" of the Merritt family. The first ore was shipped from Vermillion Iron Range to Two Harbors in August of 1884. As the train pulled out, every miner stood alongside the track and tossed in a chunk of ore for good luck. No longer active, the oldest and deepest underground mine in Minnesota at Tower-Soudan State Park near Ely offers tours into the belly of the earth where miners blasted and hand-tunneled to a ½-mile depth.

Meatball Hors d'oeuvres
"make mine ORE d'oeuvres"

1 pound ground beef
2 tablespoons cracker crumbs
1 egg, slightly beaten
½ teaspoon salt
Dash of pepper
Sauce:
2 tablespoons margarine
⅓ cup finely chopped green pepper
⅓ cup minced onion
1 (10¾-ounce) can tomato soup
2 tablespoons brown sugar
¼ cup Worcestershire sauce
1 tablespoon prepared mustard
1 tablespoon vinegar

Combine meat, crumbs, egg, salt and pepper; shape into tiny meatballs. Place in 13x9x2-inch pan and bake at 350° for about 20 minutes; drain. For sauce, combine all ingredients in saucepan. Heat to boiling, reduce heat and simmer about 20 minutes. Pour over meatballs in chafing dish. Serve hot.

Makes about 2 dozen

The Minnesota Zoological Gardens in Apple Valley is a magnificent 485 acres of open landscaping dedicated to exhibiting living organisms in their natural habitats—now more than 2000 plant species and over 1700 mammal, fish, bird, reptile and amphibian species. A monorail services the zoo, which is divided into six regions of the world including the Minnesota Trail, devoted entirely to our state. Ours is a zoo for all seasons, where winter visitors can ski scenic trails that wind amidst Siberian tigers and polar bears, and summer guests might catch an open air concert. The zoo's newest feature is the shimmering, brilliantly colored biosphere of the coral reef, a 70,000-gallon seascape replete with 4 shark varieties and thousands of tropical fish in a kaleidoscope of stripes, dots, shapes and colors. The reef can be viewed from above, or through a 53-foot window that gives a panoramic vista of this enchanted underwater world.

Marinated Shrimp
"see the sea in Minnesota"

1 onion, chopped
1 cup chopped fresh parsley
1 clove garlic, diced
1½ teaspoons salt
Dash of pepper
⅔ cup vegetable oil
⅓ cup distilled vinegar
1½ pounds shrimp

Combine all marinade ingredients; add shrimp. Marinate 24 hours, stirring often.

The state song was adopted by the legislature in 1945 from a song written by two University of Minnesota students in 1904. Here are the lyrics to *Hail! Minnesota*:

Minnesota Hail to thee!
Hail to thee our state so dear,
Thy light shall ever be
A beacon bright and clear.
Thy sons and daughters true
Will proclaim thee near and far,
They will guard thy fame and adore thy
    name;
Thou shalt be their Northern Star.

Like the stream that bends to sea,
Like the pine that seeks the blue;
Minnesota, still for thee
Thy sons are strong and true.
From thy woods and waters fair;
From thy prairies waving far,
At thy call they throng with their shout and
    song;
Hailing thee their Northern Star.

Northern Star Fish Balls

2 pounds Northern,
   filleted
½ teaspoon salt
½ teaspoon nutmeg
1 egg
2 tablespoons milk
   Vegetable oil for deep-
   frying

Grind fillets in meat grinder. Blend with salt, nutmeg and egg. Refrigerate 2 to 3 hours, until jelly-like. Add milk and shape into balls. Deep-fry until cooked through.

Makes 50 to 60

The first automobile arrived in Minnesota in 1895. In 1902, the first speeding ticket was issued in Minneapolis to Tom Shevlin, the son of a wealthy lumber baron. It seems the reckless rascal exceeded the posted limit of 10 miles per hour.

Speedy Pickled Northern
"just the ticket to keep that catch"

1 tablespoon pickling salt
½ cup sugar
1 tablespoon pickling spices
1 tablespoon concentrated lemon juice
½ cup Silver Satin white wine
1½ cups white vinegar
1 to 2 pounds Northern fillets, cut into bite-size pieces
5 medium onions, sliced

Combine all ingredients except fish and onions; bring to a boil. Boil 5 minutes; cool completely. Layer fish and onions in large glass jar. Do not pack tightly. Add liquid to cover fish; cover jar. Shake twice daily for 10 days.

Don't drive too fast south of Wadena around Hewitt and Bertha, or near Harmony and Canton because Amish horse and buggy carts still keep their unhurried pace in those areas. Nestled in various pockets of Minnesota are still cultural groups that maintain a different tempo from the rest of society. Another example is the Mennonites from Russia who live near Mountain Lake. The Amish are noted for preserving the simplicity of dress and lifestyle reminiscent of "olden days." Here is a recipe that sticks to the basics.

Bread and Butter Pickles

12 pickling cucumbers,
    thinly sliced
12 small onions
 1 green pepper
   Salt
 1 quart sugar
 1 red bell pepper
 1 teaspoon dry mustard
 1 quart diluted vinegar
 3 cups vinegar
 1 cup water
 1 teaspoon turmeric
 3 to 4 whole cloves
 1 teaspoon celery seed

Soak cucumbers, onions and green pepper overnight in salted water. Use 1 tablespoon salt to 1 quart cucumbers. Drain and rinse a little. In saucepan, mix together remaining ingredients. Bring to a boil. Add cucumber mix and bring to boiling point. Seal hot.

Makes about 2 pints

A highly-cherished and rightfully touted phenomenon of Minnesota is the easy accessibility of lakes, rivers and streams, and the happy effect it has on our lifestyle. The impressive statistic is that 95% of our population lives within 5 miles of at least one lake, river or stream. But despite the fact that Minnesotans can get wet right at home, there is still the steady flow of traffic out of the "Cities" every weekend, heading toward that hazy, indefinite destination called "Up North," "To the Cabin" or "To the Lake."

Cabin Orange Marmalade

2 large naval oranges
1 large lemon
3 cups cold water
3 cups sugar

Wash fruit; slice very thin, saving any juice. Discard seeds, core and end pieces of peel. Add 1 cup of combined fruits, peel and juice to water. In saucepan (enamel preferred), heat to boiling; boil 15 minutes. Cover; let stand overnight. In the morning, combine 3 cups of fruit mixture and 3 cups sugar. Boil rapidly about 20 minutes or to jelly stage (220°); skim. Put into sterilized jars and seal. Repeat with remaining fruit and equal amount of sugar. Serve warm over fresh biscuits, pancakes or waffles. Also excellent as glaze for ham, with baked apples, bread pudding or added to apple pie or fresh cranberry sauce.

Makes 5 pints

The Minnesota Territory was not yet two years old when it celebrated its first official Thanksgiving on December 26, 1850. Governor Ramsey chose the date, considering the day after Christmas an appropriate time to give thanks. At first, Thanksgiving Day menus consisted of anything that wasn't everyday fare. Turkeys were not included, but cranberries were. In those days, Minnesota grew enough cranberries to ship some to other states. This bountiful relish will make your taste buds thankful.

Cranberry Chutney

1 (16-ounce) package
   cranberries
2 cups sugar
1 cup water
1 cup orange juice
1 cup raisins
1 cup chopped walnuts
1 cup chopped celery
1 medium apple, chopped
1 tablespoon grated
   orange peel
1 teaspoon ground ginger

About 2 hours before serving, or up to 1 week in advance: heat cranberries, sugar and water to boiling in a 3-quart saucepan over medium heat, stirring frequently. Reduce heat to low and simmer 15 minutes. Remove from heat and stir in remaining ingredients. Cover and refrigerate.

Makes about 7 cups

cranberry

Have you ever wondered who invented puffed wheat? Have you ever wondered how to take the itch out of underwear or who Betty Crocker really is or how frozen foods stay frozen in trucks or where cellophane tape came from? If you attend the Minnesota Inventors Congress held in Redwood Falls every year, you might find the answers to these and many other burning questions which have been solved by Minnesota inventors.

Green Pepper Jelly
"a very inventive recipe"

3 large green peppers, seeded and cut up
1½ cups cider vinegar
6½ cups sugar
1 teaspoon salt
1 teaspoon cayenne pepper
1 bottle Certo
Green food coloring

Place green pepper with ½ cup vinegar in blender or food processor; chop very finely. In large saucepan, combine 1 cup vinegar, sugar, salt and cayenne. Add green pepper mixture. Bring to a boil and boil 5 minutes. Stir in Certo and food coloring; pour into sterilized jars. Seal with lids or wax. Serve with cream cheese on crackers as an hors d'oeuvre.

Makes 6 to 8 jars

The ancient art of pottery-making is being carried on by the Mdewahanton Sioux living around the old Lower Sioux Agency site near Morton. Their pottery is adorned with traditional designs, either painted on or scratched through a light overlay of slip so that the darker red clays show through. Their fine craftsmanship and faithful rendering of ancestral designs reflect an enduring tribal pride. Each symbol has meaning, and they have chosen the butterfly, which means "everlasting life," as their emblem.

Vegetable Juice

10 quarts tomatoes
 3 to 4 carrots
 1 green pepper
 5 stalks celery
 5 cups sliced onion
20 whole cloves
10 tablespoons sugar
 5 tablespoons salt
 1 tablespoon pepper
10 tablespoons lemon juice
10 tablespoons vinegar
 1 teaspoon Tabasco sauce
 1 teaspoon
   Worcestershire sauce

Wash vegetables; cut up tomatoes with skins on. Cut up carrots, green pepper and celery. (May chop in blender or food processor.) Place in large kettle with onions, cloves, sugar, salt and pepper; cover and cook until tender. Strain. Add lemon juice; vinegar, Tabasco and Worcestershire sauce to tomato juice; bring to a boil. Pour into sterilized jars and seal. Process in hot water bath 10 minutes.

Makes about 6 quarts

Note: To use remaining pulp as base for spaghetti sauce, force through strainer; add garlic, oregano and other desired spices.

Butterfly
EVERLASTING LIFE

Competitive baseball started in Minnesota in 1865. From the late 1800's until the birth of the Twins, both Minneapolis and St. Paul had professional teams, nicknamed the Millers and the Saints. Our major league team, the Minnesota Twins, played its first season in 1961. The mainstay and most popular player in the Twins' youth was Harmon Killebrew, affectionately known as "The Bashful Basher from Power Alley." While with the Twins, the "Killer" won home run titles for 5 of the 8 years from 1962 to 1969, and earned the American League's Most Valuable Player Award in 1969. Though the Twins lost the World Series in 1965 to the Los Angeles Dodgers, they avenged in 1987 when they conquered the St. Louis Cardinals. In 1991 the Twins triumphed once more, capturing the pennant over the Atlanta Braves in what will long be hailed as the most thrilling and record-breaking World Series ever. Our Twins have definitely come of age!

Harmony Eggnog
"a real killer brew"

3 eggs
6 tablespoons sugar
Dash of salt
2¼ cups evaporated milk
¾ cup water
½ cup brandy
¾ cup dark rum
1 cup whipping cream
1 tablespoon sugar
1 teaspoon vanilla
Nutmeg, optional

Prepare at least 1 day in advance of serving. In a large bowl, beat eggs lightly. Gradually beat in 6 tablespoons sugar. Stir in salt, evaporated milk and water. Stir in brandy and rum. Pour into a tightly-covered container and refrigerate 24 hours. Prior to serving, whip cream with 1 tablespoon sugar until stiff; add vanilla. Stir into eggnog mixture. Sprinkle with nutmeg.

8 servings

The North Shore Drive, alias Highway 61, hugs 150 miles of rugged lakeshore along the northern banks of Lake Superior. The drive from Duluth to Grand Portage offers many scenic opportunities to stop and gather Lake Superior agates. As rewarding as the rock-hunting is the river-scouting along this route. Numerous glittering waterfalls tumble their way to Lake Superior, and the trout and smelt fishing here is unexcelled. Among the rivers is the Temperance River, so called because it has no "bar" at the entrance. Crow Creek is sometimes called Prohibition Creek because it is nearly always dry.

Bubbly Temperance Punch
"no booze is no bar to its spirit"

1 envelope unsweetened strawberry Kool-aid
1 envelope unsweetened cherry Kool-aid
2 cups sugar
4 quarts water
1 (6-ounce) can frozen orange juice
1 (6-ounce) can frozen lemonade
1 (1-liter) bottle 7-Up
1 (1-liter) bottle Bubble-Up

Combine all ingredients except 7-Up and Bubble-Up; stir well. Just before serving, add 7-Up and Bubble-Up to taste. May also be frozen (without pop) and served as a slush, adding 7-Up or Bubble-Up when served.

Makes about 50 small glasses

Rivaling the beauty of its northern counterpart is the panoramic South Shore Drive which follows the southern part of Highway 61. It winds along the Mississippi River Valley from Red Wing to La Crescent, through scenery which varies from steep limestone bluffs and the shores of Lake Pepin to the ancient hardwood forests and the driftless areas. Because of the late frosts, this is a prolific apple-producing area, and the wide variety of trees makes the South Shore Drive a very popular route for autumn leaf-gazing. A thermos of our fragrant and tempting hot apple cider will help make your fall outing more fruitful and festive.

"Old Man River" Hot Cider

"keeps you rolling along"

2¼ cups sugar (or less)
4 cups water
2 to 2½ cinnamon sticks
8 whole allspice
10 whole cloves
1 piece crystalized ginger
4 cups orange juice
2 cups lemon juice
2 quarts apple cider or juice

Combine sugar and water in saucepan; heat to boiling and boil 5 minutes. Remove from heat; add spices, cover and let stand 1 hour. Strain; combine with juices and cider. Bring quickly to a boil. Serve hot. Can be served in mugs with a cinnmon stick in each.

Makes 4½ quarts

Amusement parks are an abiding aspect of the American way of life. Wildwood Amusement Park on White Bear Lake was advertised as "Wildwood, the Beautiful, where one may find rest, comfort, coolness and kindred delights of the good old summertime." Chicago gangsters found it appealing in the 1930's, but it met its demise with the end of the electric cars in 1938. Excelsior Amusement Park was built on Lake Minnetonka in 1925, but is also now closed. Its huge roller coaster survived, however, and continues to be a screaming success at Valleyfair in Shakopee, now Minnesota's major amusement center.

Roller Coaster Slush

½ to ¾ cup sugar
6 cups water
1 (46-ounce) can pineapple juice
2 (12-ounce) cans frozen lemonade
5 to 6 large bananas, mashed
2½ quarts 7-Up, chilled

Combine all ingredients except 7-Up; freeze in 5-quart container, stirring occasionally during freezing to prevent separation. Remove from freezer about 1 hour before serving. Fill cups about half full of slush mixture; fill with 7-Up. Top with fresh strawberries, blueberries or raspberries, if desired.

50 (½-cup) servings

Locals and tourists alike clamor to escape the menacing whine of the notorious swarms of our "Other State Bird," the ignominious mosquito. We have heard that Whitewater State Park near St. Charles is a haven from the little rascals because of its spring water. We have also heard that mosquitoes do, in fact, have merit despite their blight on our summer pleasure. They hold a valuable place in our ecological progression, gallantly feeding our myriad variety of beautiful birds. Also, an early Mankato farmer told of his dead mule being carried away by mosquitoes. That was a very helpful contribution, too. Research has shown that people build tolerance relative to a "number of bites per minute" factor. Now here is a real "Catch 22" situation. If you can catch 22 mosquitoes, you might spare yourself some bites. If you can catch 44 mosquitoes, you might spare yourself twice as many bites. However, here's the catch: according to the "bites per minute" tolerance theory, it would seem that half as many bites hurt twice as much. So, our most logical advice: either spend your summer at Whitewater State Park, or mix yourself a Brandy Slush, open all your doors and invite a few thousand of the carnivorous little beasts in to feast. That should take care of your tolerance level. It not, try another Brandy Slush as an antidote.

Brandy Slush
"with a cool sting of its own"

2 cups water
3 tea bags
1 (12-ounce) can frozen
   lemonade
1 (12-ounce) can frozen
   orange juice
6 cups water
2 cups sugar
2½ cups brandy

Make tea using 2 cups water and tea bags. Combine with remaining ingredients; freeze in 5-quart plastic container. Remove from freezer about ½ hour before serving.

About 30 (½-cup) servings

The Twin Cities consume more popcorn than anyplace else on the globe. Twin Citians like their popcorn naked, buttered or in full dress. Here are a couple of festive attires for your next batch — a capital snack in any geographic location.

Caramel Corn

2 cups packed brown sugar
1 cup margarine
½ cup light corn syrup
¾ teaspoon baking soda
¼ teaspoon cream of tartar
Dash of salt
6 to 7 quarts popped popcorn

Combine sugar, margarine and syrup in saucepan; bring to a boil and boil 5 minutes. Remove from heat and add soda, cream of tartar and salt. Stir quickly and pour over popcorn. Put in large roasting pan and bake at 200° for 1 hour, stirring occasionally. Spread on waxed paper to cool.

Makes 6 to 7 quarts

Chocolate Popcorn

2 cups sugar
2 tablespoons unsweetened cocoa powder
2 tablespoons light corn syrup
1 cup milk
2 tablespoons butter
1 teaspoon vanilla
6 to 7 quarts popped popcorn

Combine sugar, cocoa, syrup and milk in a saucepan. Cook at a rolling boil until mixture forms a soft ball when dropped into cold water (234°). Turn off heat; add butter and vanilla. Drizzle syrup mixture over popcorn, stirring constantly. Can be shaped into balls or left loose.

Gigantic statues adorn more towns in Minnesota than in any other state. From Paul Bunyan to fish to birds, these tall tale figures of plaster, stone and such catch the eye and capture the imagination of travelers. An oversized statement of the town's chosen identity, a statue is often the focal point of its festival. This map gives some indication of the variety and imagination personified by these statues.

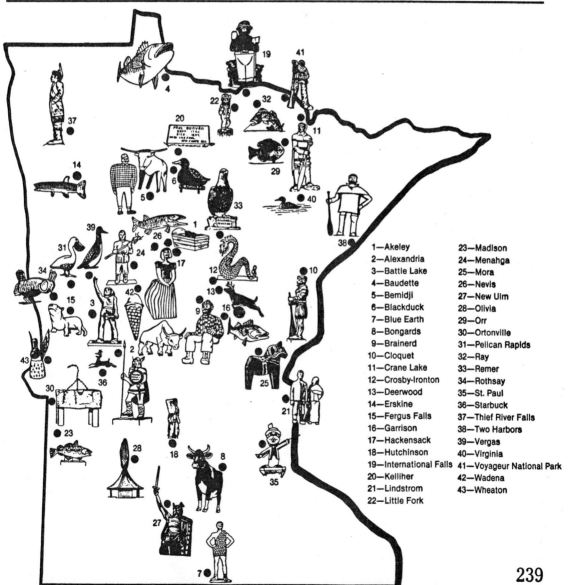

1—Akeley	23—Madison
2—Alexandria	24—Menahga
3—Battle Lake	25—Mora
4—Baudette	26—Nevis
5—Bemidji	27—New Ulm
6—Blackduck	28—Olivia
7—Blue Earth	29—Orr
8—Bongards	30—Ortonville
9—Brainerd	31—Pelican Rapids
10—Cloquet	32—Ray
11—Crane Lake	33—Remer
12—Crosby-Ironton	34—Rothsay
13—Deerwood	35—St. Paul
14—Erskine	36—Starbuck
15—Fergus Falls	37—Thief River Falls
16—Garrison	38—Two Harbors
17—Hackensack	39—Vergas
18—Hutchinson	40—Virginia
19—International Falls	41—Voyageur National Park
20—Kelliher	42—Wadena
21—Lindstrom	43—Wheaton
22—Little Fork	

General Index

S

T

Recipe Index

Recipe Index

OUR SPECIAL THANKS TO:

John Simpson and Tom, Andy and Katie Meinhover for their encouragement and endurance during another project.
Wendy and Chris Penta and Jeemer Gluesing for their injections of humor.
Mable Gluesing for accurate proof-reading and Gene Gluesing for critical input.
Mary Sazama for patient help in typesetting.

For permission to reprint information:
  Glensheen, University of Minnesota, Duluth, Minnesota
  Minnesota Wild Rice Promotion Council

For permission to reprint recipes:
  "Kerelian Steak" and "Rutabaga Casserole" — Finn Creek Museum, New York Mills, Minnesota
  "Rocks" — Glensheen Docent Council, Duluth, Minnesota
  "Scandinavian Fruit Soup" — Danebod English Ladies Aid, Tyler, Minnesota
  "Stir Fry Wild Rice, Snow Peas and Pork" and "Wild Rice Three Grain Bread" — Minnesota Wild Rice Promotion Council
  "Turkey Rissotto" — The Muffin Tin, Delano, Minnesota

For permission to reproduce drawings:
  Danebod, Tyler, Minnesota
  Glensheen, University of Minnesota, Duluth, Minnesota
  Minnesota Department of Tourism

For permission to reproduce photographs:
  Minnesota Historical Society: Divider pages for Breads, Breakfasts, Soups, Main Dishes and Vegetables
  Minneapolis Star-Journal Photo, Minnesota Historical Society: Divider page for Desserts

Numerous printed and verbal sources were used in gathering the information for this book; our thanks to all of them.

Contributors

Our special thanks to the following great Minnesota cooks who have shared their favorite recipes with us.

Adamczyk, Georgia	Perham	Fuhrken, Jack	Turtle Lake
Ahlstrom, Diane	Virginia	Funk, Mary	Wabasha
Aldrich, Joyce	Remer	Giese, Paulette	Lake George
Anderson, Barb	Albert Lea	Gillmer, Susan	Red Wing
Anderson, Adele B.	Duluth	Glommen, Sherry	Delano
Anderson, Al	Minneapolis	Gluesing, Eugene	Willow River
Anderson, Henrietta	Annandale	Gluesing, Jeanne	Minneapolis
Arnold, Kay	Walker	Gluesing, Mable	St. Paul
Arnquist, Joanne	Hoffman	Goepfert, Esther	Crosby
Arnquist, Susan	Hoffman	Goodvin, Shirley	Remer
Baana, Becky	Fergus Falls	Gould, Karla & Cary	Chaska
Bahr, Mary	Ottertail	Greenough, Betty	Frazee
Baker, Wendy	Excelsior	Grundhauser, Joanne	St. Paul
Bauck, Katy	Perham	Hafner, Pep	Slayton
Bear, Melissa	Minneapolis	Haga, Hope	Minneapolis
Beier, Sylvia	New Brighton	Hagemann, Becky	Howard Lake
Bell, Mrs. Arthur	Eagle Bend	Hagen, Lil	Pelican Rapids
Bierman, Betty	Northfield	Hagen, Linda	Hanley Falls
Boedighelmer, Linda	Wadena	Hagen-Johnson, Stephanie	Moorhead
Boo, Mary	Duluth	Hanson, Norma	Minnetonka
Bowell, Beth	St. Paul	Hawthorne, Norma	Winona
Brandt, Robin	St. Paul	Hayden, Sarah	Perham
Buising, Linda	Wadena	Hedeen, Flo	Park Rapids
Capistrant, Linda & Joe	Alexandria	Hezlep, Erin	Marshall
Carlson, Georgina	Stillwater	Hest, Bev	Hawley
Chalimonczyk, Tanya	Marshall	Holbert, Maxine	Onamia
Christensen, Cliff	New York Mills	Holman, Mary	Minneapolis
Christensen, Jean	Litchfield	Holmquist, Barb	Minneapolis
Christiansen, Marge	St. Paul	Holter, Carol	Park Rapids
Coffee, Karen	Rosemount	Homa, Kathleen & Bruce	Perham
Craft, Hazel	Park Rapids	Hoover, Kris	Perham
Crow, Bonnie	Osseo	Howe, Shari	Fulda
DeBorba, Carolyn	New Brighton	Howell, Susan Zins	Lakeland
Doughman, Don	Bemidji	Hultgren, Pat	Minneapolis
Drummond, Laura	Perham	Hunter, Donna	Moorhead
Eddy, Mary	Clearbrook	Ilstrup, Carol & Roger	Minneapolis
Ellis, Faye	Menahga	Jensen, Kay	Brainerd
Elofson, Fran	Perham	Johnson, Audrey	Perham
Erickson, Betty	Lakeville	Johnson, Betty	Faribault
Erickson, Martha	Lakeville	Johnson, Judy	Stillwater
Evert, Wendy	Sleepy Eye	Johnson, Patricia K.	Faribault
Fenner, Luci	White Bear Lake	Jones, Susan	Clearbrook
Ferris, Jeanne	Byron	Jordan, Sue	Austin
Flansburg, Donna	Mankato	Jorgenson, Amanda	Fulda
Fredenburg, Dolores	Lake Itasca	Keitel, Bill & Laurie	Worthington